West Country
FOLKLORE

Roy and Ursula Radford

Peninsula
Press

Acknowledgements

The authors would like to record their appreciation and extend thanks to all those people who encouraged them, helped with research and advised on local 'lore', including: staff of libraries in Okehampton, Holsworthy, Bodmin, Tewkesbury, Tetbury and Yeovil; members and officers of the Devonshire Association; and also Mavis Goff, Boris and Myrna Klapwald, David and Shirley Streeter, and Barrie and Brenda Tombs.

The illustrations on pages 20, 29, 37 and 63 are taken from *Thurlow's Dartmoor Companion* (Peninsula Press, 1993) and are reproduced here by kind permission of the artist, George Thurlow.

Published by Peninsula Press Ltd
P.O.Box 31
Newton Abbot
Devon TQ12 5XH

Tel: 01803 875875

Printed in England by The Cromwell Press, Trowbridge, Wiltshire.

ISBN 1 872640 41 9

Contents

Introduction:
Yesterday, Today and Tomorrow

In the West Country, memories of the Gods of Nature linger and lure, and witches pursue their ancient ways. Country cures still grow in the hedgerows; rural revels, ritual, festivals and feasts season each year, garnish every month and add taste to every day. Folklore defies time, and defies those who deny that ancient lores persist. In the western counties the Celtic yesteryear was yesterday and is today. It is as if for instance many sea-dogs who set sail from the western shores - Raleigh, Drake, Chichester, Hawkins, Grenville, Mountbatten, the Gilberts - did so this morning, as if in one brave eternal hour they slipped their moorings and sailed into worlds unknown to secure the future and forge their greater Britain.

And for those of us left at home, there is time to seek our heritage, to recognise within our own short hour a folklore known these three thousand years or more. It is a lore that survives in every town, in every field, in every street, down every lane, in every factory, on every farm, on every beach, and in every town or country cottage garden. The ritual fires of our Celtic ancestors burned on the western hills, the beacons blazed their timely warnings, the ram roast makes money for a charity, and bacon burns on a barbecue - different centuries but all linked by the lore of the flames.

Those who passed this way before us left legacies of wisdom to be explored, humour to be shared, and guidance that adds a lustre to modern life. We all carry forward to the future the rituals, customs and traditions of countless generations, and live our lives, unwittingly at times, guided by the hidden ways of the past. Age after age, through bygone centuries, folklore has been passed on down until reaching us today, varying perhaps in places, and often misunderstood. Nowhere is folklore forgotten we found; and we found it thriving in the West Country.

1 Farms and Folk

For visitors to the West Country arriving by road or rail from the North and East, or for those approaching these lands from the South or West, even the few large towns and cities that exist in the region, when first seen, remain dwarfed by the magnificent landscape that has already unfolded before the traveller's eyes. Stand in the biggest cities and it is possible to see where town and country meet, and the streets give way to green fields.

The countryside of the Western region provides Britain with some of its finest farmland, and while 'Old MacDonald' may not be found by visitors or locals, visible signs of folklore are to found in almost every field and certainly on every farm. For farmers, the well-being of their animals is of the utmost importance and, while modern farming employs modern methods, many farmers remember the old-established customs once used to ensure that the best results were achieved by the simplest methods. We met farmers across the West Country who readily admitted that they still kept to some of the old customs, but we won't necessarily reveal which ones, as we take a look at farm animal and poultry folklore.

COWS

In Dorset and Devon the weaning of calves from the cows was done on the same day of the week as the day upon which Old Christmas Day fell. The Old Christmas Day was 6 January so, whatever day of the week that was, the calves were weaned from the cows then. By weaning according to tradition the farmers considered that the calves would grow strong and would not succumb to disease or afflictions.

If a cow suffered mastitis and 'blood in the milk', the remedy proposed by the wise ones was for the farmer to take the key of a cottage door and milk the cow through the loop or bow of the key. When milking was done by hand the key could be easily held in place and the remedy was often applied.

The old Devon cure for 'bladder', a form of urticaria among cattle that causes mouths and teats to swell up, was to tie the animal's tail around a stick with a piece of string. This is still done today in some areas.

Cows suffering from 'kebbit', a tenderness between the two parts of their cloven hoof, could be cured by a Cotswold farmer taking a spade out before dawn and watching in the early hours of the morning to see where the cow, when she rose in the field, first placed her tender feet. Noting the exact hoof-marks the farmer cut out the 'scad' of turf and then replaced it, upside down. As the scad rots the foot will heal. Dartmoor farmers reckoned differently and considered that to cure 'kebble' on a cow's hoof the turf needed to be hung up in a hawthorn tree.

Feeding ash-tree leaves to cattle suffering from foot and mouth disease was a way of curing them but, if that failed, there was an alternative. It was said that the disease would respond favourably to treatment with hot cross buns. These were always baked at Easter, but were baked especially hard and dry, and then kept hung up. When they were needed, the buns were taken down and grated into milk to be fed to the suffering animals. This cure was quoted in many areas across the region as one that could be relied on.

Beside farmers, any individual fortunate enough to possess a cow took good care of it. The animal was vital to family survival, and it needed protection.

In Devon, Coryton folk considered that cattle would die if greenstuff was burned near them. A variation on this, from near Martock in Somerset, insisted that neither onion skins nor flowers were to be burned slowly in the ashes on the cottage hearth but were to be thrown directly into the flames of the fire, to avoid bringing bad luck down on any cows in calf.

For any farmer the milk yield of the animals was, and still is, a primary consideration and some of the old customs and traditions have only relatively recently died out and may still linger.

The old practice of cow shoeing was recalled by smiths and turners in St Marychurch in 1932 as having been a sure and certain way of bettering the milk yield.

Cobwebs should not be swept out of the shippen or the cows will yield less milk, and accidents will happen to the calves.

In the Teign valley it was thought that if a farmer's wife let her kettle boil dry it would cause their cows to go dry.

In Bow, it is thought that if a cow is milked not into a pail but on to the ground the cow will go dry.

Some farmers turned to nature for help by feeding balm to cows because they considered this to be an effective means of increasing milk yield. However, if cows eat putrid cabbage leaves or turnips it is said that the butter produced from their milk is offensive to the taste.

Butter is much more yellow when made from summer milk, taken when the cow is grazing on fresh grass, but during the winter, carrot juice and marigold flowers were sometimes used to colour the butter.

Buttermilk, the liquid left in the churn after the butter is made, was never refused as a drink if it was offered by a friend, or the friendship would end.

West Country wives used surplus buttermilk for making scones or bread since anything that was left after the butter had been made was no use for making good cheese.

A decoction made from boiling nettle leaves in salt water was the remedy used by farmers' wives when they needed a substitute for rennet when making cheese.

Farming is a day in, day out, all year round occupation and festivals come and go without being noticed half the time by the farmer and as far as the animals are concerned a 'saint's day' or an equinox are obviously much like one another but, somehow, it seems that Christmas is different. In the

Somerset-Devon border area it was said that cattle in their stalls kneel down at dawn on the morning of day of the birth of Christ. When the new-style year came in, the young cattle knelt on the morning of 25 December, but it was claimed that the older cattle continued to observe the Old Christmas Day.

GOATS

Information given to the Devonshire Association in 1960 suggested that some eight or nine years earlier evidence had been found indicating the sacrifice of a white goat had taken place on Bel Tor. It was claimed that people from Exeter had conducted the sacrifice. The capturing of animals on open moorland and subsequent 'ritual' or 'traditional' killings for the annual ram or ox roast is often referred to in many areas; Holne in Devon being just one. The use of goat in such events is less often recorded than that of the ox or ram and the animal is possibly regarded with some suspicion since it is widely believed that it must visit the Devil at last once in every twenty-four hours to have its beard combed.

HORSES

In all rural regions, horse owners came up with customs which they believed must be followed.

When a horse picks up a nail in its foot, causing a wound, make certain that the nail is kept. To avoid the wound festering, which could lead to the horse being destroyed, the nail must be covered in grease, wrapped and kept safe.

Don't burn onion skins at all when a mare is in foal. Bury the skins, or you'll get no colts.

Your good luck will disappear over the nearest hedge if you meet a white horse coming towards you but, if a white horse overtakes you, it has been trying to catch up with you to bring you good fortune.

Horses are said to be reliable weather forecasters. If you see one standing with its hindquarters towards the hedge, you can expect wet and rough weather.

A north Devon rhyme is one that perhaps stirs memories of sacrifice practised by Celtic peoples, in honour of Esus:

White horse, white horse,
Hung upon a tree.
White horse, white horse,
Bring good luck to me.

Still in north Devon, it is widely claimed there that an Exmoor pony has three values. It can: car [carry] whisky, zmil [smell] a pixy, an' ee wid'n cocky to a gally-bagger [shy at a scarecrow].

In Dorset and Devon, the colour of a foal's legs determined whether it would be sold by a farmer or kept for his own use. Each county had its own rhyme. In Dorset:

If your mare has a foal that has four white legs,

7

> *Keep him not even a day.*
> *If your mare has a foal that has three white legs,*
> *Sell it far away.*

Devon added:

> *A foal with two you can sell to a friend,*
> *But a foal with one you keep to its end*
> *To serve your family.*

To try to ensure that a foal with four white feet was not conceived when a stallion was brought in to service a mare the animals were coupled with the sun behind the shoulders of the stallion.

If the mare was known to 'slip her foal' the farmer would put a donkey or a goat in with her but a mare in foal would never be used to draw a funeral hearse.

Ailing horses were often treated with medicines that could also be used by the farmer; dried gentian was effective in overcoming loss of appetite or tiredness, colds could be cured with feverfew, and digestive troubles treated with nettle leaves, all of which the wise country wife used as remedies for her own family's ills.

OXEN

The ox, in Britain at least, has long since fallen from favour as a draught animal and it may be either the rosy hue of disjointed memory or the rosy hue of a local brew that prompts some older country people to claim that they recall oxen used in teams of four to pull the plough.

The animals were driven, perhaps within living memory, after being shod with iron shoes that resembled a letter 'Q', called 'queues' (the shoeing process not surprisingly referred to as 'queuing'). The plough was guided by a man or boy who maintained a steady, monotonous, drone as he worked, often using the names of the oxen in what might today be considered to be a religious-style chant. Moore, in his *History of Devonshire* notes that:

> *The tone or tune with which the driving of oxen is accompanied is*
> *mentioned by agricultural writers as remarkable and resembling the*
> *chanting of a cathedral service.*

He considered it not improbable that the practice might have originated in the Roman Catholic service to which people were formerly much attached. The ploughboy provided the tenor voice while the ploughman chanted the lower notes, all of which was supposed to animate the team of oxen. "Nowhere," Worth suggests," is so much cheerfulness observed in ploughing, as in Devonshire. The team is said to stop when the chanting ceases."

Like cows, oxen are said to recognise Christmas by falling on their knees before the manger - but at midnight on Christmas Eve, rather than dawn on Christmas Day.

PIGS

For many West Country people pigs were not just any old animal, but were the great providers - almost a friend of the family at times, and made welcome when they arrived. A pig was always put into its new home backwards so as to avoid bad luck.

Cornish pigs, it is believed, sleep soundest when the wind blows, while in the Cotswolds pigs are said to be able actually to 'see' the wind. According to custom, if you look at the tail of a pig you will see the direction of the wind indicated by the curl of their tail.

In the olden days the local parson would be given the gift of a 'suckling pig', in addition to the 'tithe-pig', so that he would bless the house, animals and crops to ensure plenty.

Pigs should not be slaughtered on Good Friday; and killing them when the moon is on the wane must also be avoided, otherwise there will be problems with curing the meat or keeping it.

To get full value from it, a pig should be killed a day or so before the full moon; during this period it will weigh heavier than if it is killed when the moon is on the wane.

The ghost of Judge Jeffreys, the 'Hanging Judge', still visits the old court-room in Lydford, Devon, where, according to local legend, he appears in the shape of a black pig. Around the area it is said that a black pig will appear to anyone who has been ill-wished by the spirit of Judge Jeffreys.

There is a belief in Dorset that the six little holes on the inside of each of the knuckles of a pig's foreleg were made by the Devil's claw when he caught the animals trying to escape from his herd of swine and forcibly dragged them back.

POULTRY

Poultry have always been among the great providers for country dwellers. To ensure a good hatching, it was the custom in parts of Gloucestershire to set a broody hen on thirteen eggs on the thirteenth day of the month with the hope of hatching more hen chicks than cockerels. In Dorset it was considered unlucky to set a hen on an even number of eggs, and that the right way to set the bird was to tuck her head under her right wing and swing her around until she fell asleep and could then be put on her clutch of eggs most easily.

It was said in mid-Devon that the sign of the Cross should be marked on the eggs beneath a sitting hen to ensure that the Devil could not get at them. A more practical purpose for the sign might have been to check that the hen had turned the eggs over each day.

Egg sexing was always an important country practice and still is today, with many people using the tried and tested traditional methods. A pendulum, consisting of a needle attached to a long woollen thread, is dangled over the freshly laid eggs to determine their fertility. Only if the egg was fertile did the needle move, in a circular motion if there was to be a hen and across the egg if a cockerel was forthcoming.

It was widely recognised that this system would also work on women and we personally recall a similar method employed in the late 1940s by a farmer's wife to determine the sex of the baby that a neighbour was expecting. The pendulum went in all directions, to the consternation of the pregnant lady and the enjoyment of her young relatives. The farmer's wife had the last laugh though. She was right for twins arrived - a boy and a girl, just as predicted. For other ladies, at other times, the farmer's wife was right again; three times to our knowledge.

Poultry, thankfully, are still a common sight in the countryside, scratching around the farmyard or pecking in the field near a cottage; and there are many folk still who watch them for their powers of prediction.

A crowing hen was often killed off immediately because it was regarded as unlucky at least and as an omen of death at worst. In Shepton Mallet we came across the couplet:

A whistling woman and a crowing hen
Will summon Old Harry out of his den

while the Dorchester version was:

A whistling woman and a crowing hen
Are good for neither God nor men.

A cockerel that is heard crowing at night in Dorset is said to be foretelling the death of a person while the night-crowing cockerel in Devon is warning of wet weather approaching:

If uz 'ears a cock a crowin' a-bed
'E'll wake uz at dawn wi' a watery head.

The afternoon crowing of the cockerel which foretells of death was remembered by Thomas Hardy and included in his novel *Tess of the D'Urbervilles.*

If a cockerel near Cirencester crowed after sunset, some awful calamity was expected to occur, and if a hen crowed at all its head would be cut off immediately to stop it doing the Devil's bidding and bringing disaster to the family.

A crowing cockerel however is normal in the countryside, though sometimes placed at risk nowadays by those who have no ear for country life. A cockerel, looking in your door and crowing, is trying to tell you that a stranger is about to call, while one crowing outside in the middle of the day is bidding welcome to a visitor, except in Torquay where, if a cockerel crows at all, it is said to be clearing up the weather.

Cockerels will crow all night before Christmas Day to bid 'each fettered ghost slip to his several grave'.

SHEEP

A young Devon maid, wishing to know how long it would be before she would wed, was advised that she should count the first lambs she sees. Their number will equal the years she must wait.

When walking or riding in the countryside take particular note when approaching sheep of the first lamb you see. If it is looking towards you, it will bring you good luck.

A rhyme from Gidleigh warns farmers that:

If your flock begins to blacken
Your luck then begins to slacken.

Not far distant, a farmer nowadays specialises in breeding black sheep, presumably profitably.

If he notes local custom, he won't burn onion skins during lambing though, or he'll have bad luck with his flock.

Remembered for his help to farmers at the beginning of this century was a snake-charmer named Kelland, who lived between Yealmpton and Plympton, and who could, at a distance and with no physical contact, staunch the flow of blood from lambs when their tails were cut off.

To the West Country of yesteryear sheep were of vital importance, much more than in the North of England where the mills were at the forefront of economic development. In the South and West the rural work was less arduous when:

With the rose and the lily and the daffodowndilly
The lads and the lasses a sheepshearing go.

Thomas Hardy's vision of country work has a poetic pastoral hue that might not have been readily recognised by the men and women who faced the back-breaking work of shearing.

When the hard work was over, the sheep-shearing festivities got under way, with Christmas pudding served that had been saved six months for the purpose. The wish of the workers was that, come next year, there would be work a'plenty again:

Here's a health to all the flock, pray God increase the woolly stock,
Born twenty where there's now born ten, so maids and men can shear again.

And back to the fields went the West Country shepherds:

Here's a health unto the shepherd,
Tending to his dumb creatures
As they feed on the hill and the field;
And with other dumb creatures
Their fruit do they yield;
For their dung serves the corn ground
And their wool clothes the poor;
So drink up your cider, then fill up some more.

A STOLEN SHEEP - AND A HANGING MAN

Sheep stealing has always been a problem for Devon farmers. Once they received unusual help.

Norman, the Brigand of Broad Down, maintained a lucrative living by stealing anything that he could lay his hands on to sustain, some say, at least one wife and an ever-expanding brood of youngsters. His speciality, and most rewarding activity, was sheep stealing.

As he strode across Broad Down, not caring if he was observed, few travellers crossed his path, but many a farmer was wary of him. When Norman was around, they could almost be certain that livestock would be lost. However, whenever his solid figure was seen striding the Devon turf between Colyton and Wiggaton, or Sidbury and Shute, those who observed him swore that he was never seen to carry anything with him. Never did he appear to possess the means to secure a stolen animal.

Sheep, always timid creatures, would be startled by anyone stumbling across the uneven ground where stealth was not possible and would swiftly elude any pursuer, lawful or otherwise, across the rutted landscape where only a dog might be a match for them. It is certain however that Norman was never seen to be accompanied by a dog, yet he never passed by without a farmer finding that his flock had been reduced.

Only through the strange manner in which he met his end was Norman's secret revealed. Late one dry summer afternoon, after a day's back-breaking work in the fields, a very tired and thirsty farmer was wending his way homeward to Southleigh. He still had a long way to go but his gaitered step faltered when his attention was taken by the strange, occasional bleating of a seemingly straying sheep whose cries echoed pityingly from an outcrop of stone.

Having determined where the sounds were coming from, the farmer stopped, dropped his tools and empty cider cask beside the track, and turned off it to attend to the animal's plight. The weakening sun hung low in the sky but perspiration pouring from the farmer's brow forced him to stop occasionally to clear his eyes with the back of his hand as he clambered across the uneven coarse turf towards the outcrop in an attempt to find the stricken animal.

Led astray at first by false echoes the farmer searched until eventually, on sloping ground near a projecting rock, he found the sheep tethered by a line pulled taut, up and across the stone then down again to the swinging, swaying body of the man that many feared but need fear no more. As the terror-stricken sheep tried to scramble down the slope, the hanging man was dancing a jig of death.

Sweating and straining, the farmer summoned sufficient strength to pull the struggling sheep back up the slope to ease the rope behind him. The dead man's body dropped to the ground below the protruding stone and, released from the rope at last, the sheep scurried away.

Norman's protruding, unseeing eyes stared towards the distant sea as the farmer unwound the hempen cord that bit deep into the dead man's neck. Taking care to avoid the stare of death as he removed the rope completely, the man found that the thief had secured it tightly around his own waist. Concealed beneath his rough jerkin, the rope had not been an obvious addition to his figure, and had left his hands free, but was always readily available to secure a stolen sheep. Until one unwitting animal became hangman to the thief.

Norman, having captured his quarry, must have paused at the rock, possibly either to rest himself or to calm the sheep by permitting it to graze at the end of its tether. Perhaps the tired thief then dozed in the summer sun, his prize secure, the sheep safely attached to him. Surveying the area now, some say in order to seek for greener grass, the sheep must have circled around the sleeping figure, looping running rope round Norman's neck. However it happened, and the entire truth will never be fully known, the sheep eventually managed to reach a point above the rogue who slept to stand alone on the protruding stone.

Free from the restraining grasp of the slumbering sheep stealer, either tempted by the greener grass or through trying to escape, the animal leapt from the rock and the rope jerked tight, throttling the thief as he was dragged on high. On the other side of the stone, the rope remained secured around the shoulders of the sheep.

The animal, as it struggled to escape, jerked on the rope with increasing frenzy while the throttling thief must have desperately pawed the air in a final but failing attempt to save his own life.

The projecting rock soon became known locally as 'Hangman's Stone', and its name might have become attributed to some other origin but for a simple burial place about half a mile due west of the rock. The burial spot is a continual reminder to all those who pass by of the stealer of sheep who was hanged on the rock by a stolen sheep and is known, most significantly and definitively, as Norman's grave.

2 Cottage Garden Folklore

The vision of a country cottage garden, filled with flowers from spring to summer's end, vegetables growing in neat rows, trees and bushes bearing blossom and fruit, remains in the mind of visitors long after they have returned to their own home. And in those gardens with their seasonal produce is nurtured the lore that still guides.

Beans have always been an important crop and there are many customs concerning their planting. In his 1750 edition of *Modern Husbandman*, William Ellis wrote, 'Sow beans in the mud, and they'll grow like wood.' It has also been suggested that four beans need to be sown to get one to harvest:

One for the pigeon, one for the crow,
One to rot, and one to grow.

A Devon squire is reported early this century to have always insisted his gardener should stop whatever he was doing when he heard the first cuckoo and rush off immediately to plant his French beans.

Broad beans however need to be in the ground long before the cuckoo's cry can be heard. Some West Country customs call for them to be planted on 21 December, St Thomas's Day, and there are many who follow the Cotswold custom of getting them into the ground before Christmas, even if the planting day is not defined. This is in contrast to the colder north of England where the advice was:

On St Valentine's Day,
Beans should be in the clay.

In the cottage garden, beans have a wholesome reputation, but they posses a more sinister side. Today 'pick your own' purchasing has become popular and town and country dwellers alike tramp the fields to take a crop but, well within living memory, beanfields were something that many people kept well away from. They were said to be the 'harbour of the dead', where the souls of the recently departed resided, waiting for an opportunity to capture a new life from any foolish mortal who entered into their domain. Youthful adventurers who scoffed at such superstition were challenged to sleep overnight in the beanfield among the dead and departed. Any who did so faced the prospect of experiencing terrifying dreams that would send them raving mad. Incidentally, do remember to plant beans upside down in leap years.

A bean it is claimed is an effective deterrent where witches are concerned and bean bullets can repel the attack of a witch as effectively as silver bullets. Spat out at a witch, a spittle-coated bean can inflict fatal wounds and in the remote rural areas of some counties a person who will not eat beans, simply claiming not to like them, is still often regarded with suspicion.

While some consider that eating it is an anti-social activity, garlic is regarded universally as an aphrodisiac of high repute and has valuable medicinal properties. In Somerset it is valued for preventing witches casting their evil eye on a victim. Gardeners use it to move moles; the creatures apparently fail to recognise the aphrodisiac qualities attributed to the garlic by the humans and distance themselves from their mole-mate.

Jove's beard, as the fleshy houseleek plant was also known, flourished on cottage and house roofs rather than in the garden. Since Celtic days, houseleek on the roof was recognised as providing protection against witches, fire and lightning. On the ground it was sometimes considered to be an unlucky plant, unless garden leeks were grown nearby. Pulling it out and throwing it away was frowned upon since such action would bring marital upheaval in its wake.

Lettuce is a favoured salad base today but in country gardens it was once regarded as an awesome intruder. It was a 'sterile' plant, much feared by many maidens. They were not encouraged to eat it since it could, if eaten without salt added, have very undesirable effects and could be a cause of a woman's infertility.

The popularity of lettuce improved towards the end of the last century, however, when it was suggested that it aroused a desire for lovemaking and would counteract the effects of too much wine. We have friends who confirm the latter.

Parsley was considered in Devon and Cornwall to be an evil plant that, if it was introduced to the garden, would ensure that someone in the family died within the year. Folk in Somerset feared transplanting parsley, in case they then had to bury a relative or friend. If someone did have the courage to add it to their garden, the neighbours might have taken a keen interest in whether or not the plant took to its new home. A parsley plant which wouldn't grow was taken to be clearly indicating the presence of the Devil, who was residing in the same plot of ground and was enjoying the values of the plant; from below.

Despite it being a delicacy that delights the Devil, and having a reputation for predicting death, parsley remains a popular herb which Totnes gardeners claim to achieve better results with by planting it on Good Friday. Mixing the seeds with coal dust helps it grow.

In any case, according to custom in Wimborne, parsley seeds should be planted with a spoon, to stop the electricity of the body running through them and retarding their growth. Even when it does grow well, in Wimborne it is said of the plant that it goes to visit the Devil three times before it comes up.

According to the general West Country maxim, no matter how good a gardener is, "Parsley won't grow where missus is maister", but people in the district of Clovelly know better. There it is claimed that parsley grows best at a home where the woman is boss.

It is hard to believe nowadays that the potato was once regarded as an aphrodisiac or that the root at one time fetched £300 a pound because of this.

The ancient custom of carrying a potato as a remedy for rheumatism probably still remains one of the most widely practised West Country and even country-wide folk-remedies.

Gardeners can always be relied upon to have a rhyme for any reason and any crop in any season. Peas like beans were part of the everyday diet and so the lore of planting them properly is plentiful. Lunar lore led the way for centuries, and it still does for many a town or country gardener who takes note of what Thomas Tusser wrote in *Redivus*:

> Sow peas and beans in the wane of the moon,
> Who soweth them sooner, he soweth too soon.

To forecast a good crop, or prepare for a bad one, present-day pea planters need only use their powers of observation at the right time:

> On Candlemas day if the thorns hang adrop,
> Then you are sure of good pea crop.

A good crop was celebrated in Cornwall on 'Peasen Monday', the Monday before Shrove Tuesday, with the custom of eating pea-soup.

Pea-soup was popular with most people, but not with one old farmer from Lower St Columb who just did not like the taste of the stuff. Threatened once with a celebratory pea-soup meal being prepared by his wife he suddenly recalled an important reason that required him, without delay, to ride some distance on horseback to the next village to see some farmers there. He departed that morning with a smile on his face and returned at nightfall looking grim. His wife offered to warm up the remains of the pea-soup for him but he stormed off saying that wherever he had gone that day his friends had insisted on sharing their pea-soup with him, and he liked it even less now than before.

Once the crop was in, there was more to look forward to than just a meal. For a maiden to find nine peas in a pod was considered to be very fortunate for with the help of the pod her future could be revealed. She knew that on a tiny piece of paper she must write, "Come in, my dear, And do not fear", then enclose the scrap of paper safe inside the pod and place it beneath the door. Patience was then sorely tested as she waited and watched for the first girl, of a similar age to herself, to enter the through the door. The initial letter of the first name of the first such girl to pass through the portal would reveal the initial of the name of the man the maiden would marry.

Rhubarb makes exceedingly good pies, crumbles and tarts, goes well with custard and is one of summer's culinary delights. It is also found in most country gardens.

It does possess many other values and Culpeper wrote that rhubarb "provides remedies for ear-ache, tooth-ache, jaundice, the king's evil, urinary troubles, dimness of sight, ulcerous sores, and inflammation".

If rhubarb runs to seed very quickly it denotes a death or trouble in the family.

Sage was the cottage garden herb that symbolised domestic virtue. It flourishes best in a Cornish garden where the mistress is master of the house, and grows best for those who are wise. Timid Devonian men were known to cut down healthy sage bushes for fear of being mocked by their neighbours:

If the sage tree thrives and strongly grows
The master's not master, so everyone knows.

Sage in Somerset was a herb that promised to promote good health if eaten in quantity, at the right time:

They who would live for ever and a day,
Must eat their fill of sage in May.

It is a herb which custom there decreed would flourish while the master of the house was in good health but withered if he was sick or ailing. (T'other way round in Wiltshire.) John Evelyn, in his seventeenth-century manual on arboriculture, proclaimed the plant possessed so many wonderful properties that "the assiduous use of it was said to render men immortal".

For gardeners the sage plant stimulated the growth of rosemary and rue and, if planted among cabbages, protected them from being attacked by the cabbage-white butterfly.

If that pest proved too much of a headache, an early headache tablet was compounded from a spikenard of sage, together with toasted seeds of the herb, powdered and mixed and bound with the plant's own juice.

Banks on which the wild thyme grew once abounded in the West Country and the souls of the dead are said to reside in the flowers of thyme, particularly the tormented souls of murdered men.

Its presence in a garden is a symbol of strength for it is a herb loved by both bees and fairies. Members of some friendly societies and similar organisations carry sprigs of thyme at funerals and throw them into the grave of a dead member.

Among its many medicinal uses it is said to be effective in killing off worms in the belly, and assisting a speedy delivery for women in the labour of childbirth.

Devil's plaything and Devil's rattle, the West Country alternative names for yarrow, give some indication of its alternative uses also. Picked not from a garden but from a young man's grave on the night of a full moon, the plant is a powerful aid when used for casting spells, in divination, or working witchcraft.

To determine which friendships should be developed, an ounce of yarrow sewn up in flannel and placed beneath the pillow will induce a dream of clarification if accompanied by the words of the charm:

Thou pretty herb of Venus tree,
Thy true name it is Yarrow,
Now who my bosom friend must be,
Pray tell thou me tomorrow.

Yarrow has many uses: strewn on the threshold of your home you can rely upon the herb to keep witches at bay; worn upon the child or tied to its cot or cradle it protects a baby; hung up in the home on St John's Eve it keeps illness away for a year; and eaten at a wedding it ensures seven years of love, at least.

Caring for the cottage garden is an all-year-round occupation and during the work the gardener will find other 'friends' among the plants - ants for instance. Ants arouse curious conflicts in people; their presence in the larder of a cottager or kitchen of a king is likely to call forth every remedy available to dispose of them while their proverbial industry, social structure and family instincts are held up as worthy examples to humans.

In many areas in the West Country it is considered wrong if a colony of ants is destroyed, and the perpetrator of such an evil deed invites ill fortune to attend them.

Ants are sometimes considered to be the remains of a fairy tribe, some of the 'little people' who once populated this planet, and their present state is said to be indicative of their fall from grace.

Despite all this, and the wisdom that could be gained from them, we humans generally prefer to live decidedly separate lives, removing them from our presence whenever we can, by whatever means is available.

Oliver Cromwell has been held responsible for a considerable amount of damage caused to churches, including the destruction of stone figures, religious masonry and church items. Ants however probably caused more destruction to church figurines and symbolic masonry, not by what they did to the stonework but because of what the stonework was supposed to do to the ants. Saintly stone relics could be relied upon to repel them, or so it was once thought, and at Coryton, powder obtained by grinding down the figures or statues of saints was sprinkled on doorsteps, in barns, on gates and on paths to keep the ants away. This custom was not unknown in many other parts of the West Country where the ground stone was also used in compounds and concoctions to be rubbed on or consumed, as required, to cure illnesses and all manner of complaints.

In 1714 John Gay most adequately described in 'Shepherd's Week' a Devon custom that could still be tried today. It is a way to 'charm' a lover with that garden foe, the snail:

> Last May-day fair I search'd to find a snail,
> That might my secret lover's name reveal.
> Upon a gooseberry bush a snail I found
> For always snails near sweetest fruit abound.
> I seiz'd the vermine, home I quickly sped,
> And on the hearth the milk-white embers spread.
> Slow crawl'd the snail, and if I right can spell,
> In soft ashes mark'd a curious L:
> Oh, may this wondrous omen lucky prove!
> For L is found in Lubberkin and Love.
> With my sharp heel I three times mark the ground,
> And turn me thrice around, around, around.

At Sandford, a cottage dweller earlier this century, plagued with caterpillars in her garden, resorted to an ancient method of ridding herself of the infestation that was reducing the cabbages and green-stuff to skeletons. She spiked one of the caterpillars on a long knitting needle, and roasted it in front of the fire. Next morning there was not a caterpillar to be found in the garden.

It is a long-standing belief that insects will be frightened away by their own kind being burnt.

Some other garden residents just were not welcome. Newts were often considered to be poisonous and to possess the ability to spit fire. They were also blamed for killing animals. Near Cornworthy, any mysterious death of cattle in the district was blamed upon the newts in the ponds from which the animals drank.

Dandelion is a common herb all too often condemned as a weed even by cottage gardeners. The French and Dutch consume leaves in the spring, whereas most of their West Country cousins regard them as a treat for pet rabbits.

Dandelions are welcomed by beekeepers at the end of winter as they provide bees with fresh food, and give a valuable springtime boost to honey production.

Dandelion leaves boiled in a little water with stinging nettles and watercress make a tonic which, when drunk, is reputed to keep away all illness.

For centuries country women have collected dandelion roots in the autumn, dried them thoroughly and roasted them in an oven until they are crisp enough to crumble. Boiled water added to the roast, crushed root produces a pleasant drink.

Picked on St John's Eve, dandelion flowers hung in bunches around doors and windows are a very powerful witch repellent.

THE DEVON BUTTERFLY

There was, it seems, a somewhat unpleasant superstition, long standing in south Devon that advised people of the necessity to kill the first butterfly they saw if they wished to avoid ill-fortune settling on their shoulders throughout the coming year. On 14 May 1825, *Woolmer's Exeter and Plymouth Gazette* contained an item that referred to the custom.

A gentleman and his daughter, walking to church, were overtaken by a young man running at speed. They stepped aside, not wishing to impede his progress if he was running after someone, and watched his frantic pursuit, though they couldn't identify his quarry. The man and maid continued on their way and soon afterwards caught up with an elderly gentleman of their acquaintance. They realised that the young man in a hurry was this man's son. "He came past in such a rush," the girl explained to the old man, "that we failed to recognise who it was." The three of them continued on their way and walked together towards the church as the old man explained that his son had been chasing the first butterfly they had seen, to make sure that he killed it. The men came to a halt when the girl stopped and let go of her father's hand.

"Why would he want to kill a butterfly?" she asked.

"So that we will avoid the misfortunes that will befall us if he fails to do so," the old gentleman replied as he moved on again.

Taking his daughter by the hand the man led her onwards towards the church where, at its gates, they found the young man proudly displaying a dead butterfly and saying to all who passed by, "I caught 'en at last." The girl averted her face as she passed by the trophy while her father made some comment to the young man regarding the unpleasant superstition.

"Ah, zir," came the reply, " but oi knows the consequences of ignorin' it. Wan year I didn't kill the first but'fly I zeed, and didn' I 'ave wundrous bad luck for the whole year !"

3 Country Companions

For country dwellers, bees and their produce have long been important.

For centuries, honey not only added sweetness to food but was used as a medicine and a treatment for wounds. Today, while bees' role in pollination is possibly underestimated by many people, the value of honey is universally recognised, beeswax is widely used, and the benefits to be gained from propylis, a 'gluey' bee product, are being researched by scientists.

For most keepers of bees, it is a privilege to spend their time with the creatures, enjoy the communities the bees create, and share the honey the bees provide. Honey is always 'shared' since every good beekeeper ensures that the bees keep all they need.

'Sharing' is the all-important custom, and a close relationship grows between the keepers and their bees.

Like country people for centuries past, beekeepers regularly keep their bees aware of things that happen to the family or to friends. When a death of a family member or friend occurs it is the custom that bees are advised and put into mourning with their hives adorned with black crepe, wool or ribbon. We learned of this custom from a retired lady, Miss Dorothy Flowers, a well-known beekeeper in Sticklepath who at the time was chairperson of the Okehampton Branch of The Devon Beekeepers Association and who encouraged us to keep bees, encouragement for which we remain grateful. The custom was still current at the time of her death in August 1994. When the beekeeper themself dies, the bees must be allowed to mourn.

The 'telling' tradition probably arose from the fact that the keeper of bees for the village or community was the only one with the knowledge and experience to handle them. If they died without having trained someone to follow in their footsteps, the bees could be neglected and allowed to die because of disease or through lack of winter food. To the community, however, it might appear that the bees had pined away, missing their keeper.

Beekeepers can still be found who 'share' bees, keeping to the custom of not taking money for them since bees should be 'given'. Beekeeping has become a modern industry, but where just a few hives are cared for by a beekeeper the old traditions survive.

"A swarm of bees in May, is worth a load of hay" is the Dorsetshire opening to a well-known rhyme but in Cornwall the worth is "a yow [ewe] and lamb same day".

In the Sourton area, where they know a good thing when they see it, the variation was, "A swarm of bees in May, is worth a guinea that very day". As the swarm would produce honey to share that very year, it was the equivalent of a guinea in the pocket.

A beekeeper coming upon a swarm provided by the God of Nature recognises good fortune even in July when "it isn't worth a fly" for it will be valuable the next year.

According to a beekeeper we met once in the sixteenth century Ship Inn at Ugborough, a swarm of bees can be settled by ringing bells. As beekeepers we still wonder whether our friend was influenced at the time by the Bell's behind the bar.

A swarm of bees in flight is a wonderful sight, but a frightening one for some people. Contrary to what some might say, bees *will* sting when they settle in a swarm so stay clear, don't disturb them and call in a beekeeper, not an exterminator. The police, or library, will probably know of local beekeepers.

Gerard's *Herball* and Cornish lore both advise that if the hives of bees are rubbed with leaves of the herb balm this will cause the bees to keep together and cause others to come to them. Pliny recommended balm to be used to call home straying bees. Lemon balm rubbed into a new hive will make bees settle in their new home.

According to Somerset custom, beehives should only be moved on Good Friday, and in Cornwall it is said that the collection of honey from the hives should take place on 24 August, St Bartholomew's Day, the day of the patron saint of beekeepers.

If you want to test out one very special West Country belief, go to visit the bees at Christmas. It is said bees sing in their hives at midnight on Christmas Eve. According to legend they hum the hundredth psalm, 'O make a joyful noise unto the Lord'.

On 8 March 1883 a letter was published in the *Daily News* that had been received from the Reverend J Hoskyns Abrahall, who resided at Coombe Vicarage near Woodstock and who wrote:

> A friend of mine, who is a vicar of St Cleer, in East Cornwall, has
> told me that at least one housemaid of his - I think his servants in general

- very anxiously avoided killing a spider, because Parson Jupp, my
friend's predecessor [whom he succeeded in 1844], was, it is believed,
somewhere in the vicarage in some spider - no one knew in which of
the vicarage spiders.

Some people will simply not kill a spider even if they fear them.

According to Cornish belief, one reason for spiders often escaping the death penalty is that a spider spun its web above Christ in the manger, concealing him completely and hiding him from Herod.

Cat lovers of the world unite in their devotion to their furry friends but the domestic cat hasn't always been welcome in the home.

"Cats and children never thrive together", is a Devon saying so, if your children are regularly taken ill, try selling the cat.

In north Devon it is still held by some that a kitten and a baby should not share the same home because it is unlucky for them to do so.

Careful parents today will take every precaution to ensure that a cat can't get near a sleeping babe in case it should settle down on the child's face and smother it but cats have long been considered able to suck the breath of babies and thereby cause their death. The *Annual Register* of 25 January 1791 contains the following comment:

A child of eighteen months old was found dead near Plymouth; and it
appeared on the Coroner's inquest that the child died in consequence
of a cat sucking its breath, thereby occasioning a strangulation.

It is widely believed in the West Country that a cat will not remain in a house wherein lies a corpse and many cats have been known to 'disappear' when a death has occurred in a household, only to reappear after the funeral has taken place.

The cat which refuses to come into its own house in Cornwall is one that can sense someone in it is going to die.

In farming communities generally, not just in Devon, the cat had work to do and was not an animal that would be cosseted indoors. In a farmhouse at close of day, a good wife would entreat her household, "Now then, boys to bed, and cats to barn".

When seeking a cat, look to see if there is a tabby kitten marked with a letter 'M' on its head. That one will turn out to be a good mouser.

Cats born in May are not good mousers and will, quite likely, bring snakes, slow-worms, and other reptiles into your house at every opportunity but a 'blackberry' cat, one born near Michaelmas, can be expected to be mischievous and playful all through its life.

A cat that is regularly fed makes the best mouser since it hunts for sport not for food, while a cat that hunts through hunger will gorge itself then lie down and go off to sleep.

Herrick, in his 'Hesperides', writes:

True calendars, as pussies eare,
Wash't o're to tell what change is near

and in 1643 John Swan, in his *Speculum Mundi,* wrote of the cat, saying that:

She useth therefore to wash her face with her feet, which she licketh
and moisteneth with her tongue; and it is observed by some that, if she
put her feet beyond the crown of her head in this kind of washing, it is
a signe of rain.

Dogs often appear in West Country ghost stories, with dogs or phantom dogs appearing in different places. The more fleshy hound of the Baskervilles has done wonders for Dartmoor and is regularly read of, while Somerset's black beast of Budleigh Hill is a phantom more often seen. A local sexton once explained that regular 'presence'of the dog came about as the result of an unusual accident that occurred before a burial.

A coffin being carried from Horner Mill to Selworthy was accidentally dropped when one of its handles inexplicably came loose. The bearers put the coffin on the ground and tried to secure the coffin-handle by knocking it back in place with a stone. As the handle nails were banged into the coffin, one pierced the skull of the dead person contained inside and their spirit escaped.

Never having reached the church or received its final blessing, the wayward spirit still roams the Budleigh area, denied eternal salvation, condemned to retain the guise of a dog and is regularly, reliably, seen.

It is believed in many West Country counties that a dog looking out of the window presages the arrival of a friend, but that a dog howling inside a house in a mournful manner is aware that its owner, or a near relation, is about to die.

Donkeys in any field are sure to attract attention but it should be remembered that if anyone sits on the ground where a donkey has been rolling around, they will be followed by evil when they walk away from the place.

THE CURSE OF FLEAS

Fleas are not the most favoured or welcome insect, but there is a West Country custom that offers some protection from the intruder. Windows should not be opened on 1 March as this causes fleas to swarm into the house.

This was not however sufficient to help a farmer and his wife from Bow in Devon when their house was suddenly plagued by fleas in great quantities. No matter what they did or what remedy they tried neither the farmer nor his good lady could get rid of the invading hordes so the farmer resolved to apply to a white witch for help. He made a respectful approach to the powerful personage, and was pleased to be invited to attend the witch in person. The farmer hurried to the man's house (not all witches are women), and upon entering the door of the premises made his abeyances to the figure that sat in a brightly lit window seat staring through the glittering glass before him. The witch took no notice of the man and continued to gaze out of his window and across the countryside. The farmer, who had previously had little to do with witches, waited patiently, sometimes moving his weight awkwardly from one foot to the other with enough noise to ensure that the witch was aware of his presence. The witch continued to ignore him.

"Could I just tell..." the farmer began to stutter at last, unable to contain his patience any longer.

The witch's head moved with but the slightest negative inclination, though the farmer later swore that the head turned full circle, and the man's words seemed to be strangled in his throat.

"There is no need," snapped the witch, without moving his gaze from some distant outdoor object. "I know why you have come to me." The farmer's jaw dropped as the witch continued to speak without so much as glancing in his direction. "The one who 'overlooked' [gave the 'evil eye'] you also knows that you were coming here to gain my help. Return to your home now. Go straight there without any delay or diversion. You will find your wife and your dwelling rid of all the fleas. Go straight home, do you hear."

The farmer attempted to form words of agreement and thanks but not a single sound escaped his lips as the witch raised just one finger to dismiss him from his powerful presence. The bewildered man hastened away to do exactly as he was bid and ignored friends he passed on the road who invited him to stop and talk or take food with them. On arriving home he was greeted by a grateful wife: the plague of fleas had gone.

A final thought for those who find fleas offensive. It is said that fleas never infest a person who is near to death.

4 Meadows and Fields

Everywhere across the West Country the folklore of centuries can be found every day, in every location.

When you are travelling through Devon and you happen to see a hare crossing your path shortly after you have started out on your journey you are advised to turn back. It has long been known in the county that such an encounter will mean, at the very least, that your travels will lead you to bad luck. If in Cornwall though, observe any hare you see in meadow, field or moor very carefully to determine its colour. Maidens who are deceived by unfaithful lovers and who die of a broken heart are said to roam the land, shape-shifted at death into the form of a white hare. Take extra care if the hare seems kindly disposed to you and draws near. The undead maiden is said to be seeking her betrayer to take his life and release her soul.

Wild Harris of Kenegie House, a gentleman from the parish of Gulval near Penzance, was killed when out hunting. He fell from his horse when it was frightened by the earth-bound spirit of a betrayed maiden who appeared in its path in the guise of a white hare.

In Dorset, it is much worse if an encounter with a hare takes place at dusk.The hare might be a shape-shifting witch that has taken animal form, hunting the downs and hills at night for travellers to harm. Only a silver bullet can have any affect on such a creature and as very few commuters, past or present, carry such protection, turning back makes sense again. Why risk confronting a witch?

Steer clear also of residences in Somerset around which white hares have been seen. The appearance of a white hare near a house is a sure sign that death will visit the next person who calls at the house.

Moretonhampstead folk once thought that if a rabbit or hare was seen running through the streets it was a sign that a fire would break out. Death accompanied the appearance of wild white rabbits in the area, swiftly visiting those who saw them.

In Dorset a meal of rabbit brains was considered to be enough to soothe any troublesome child and to satisfy or stifle their 'longing' for something the parent could not provide. *Notes and Queries* of 1885 recorded that a woman in Lyme Regis when failing to deal with her restless, fractious child sought guidance from a wise person who lived in the town. The advice she received was that her child would never be well until it had eaten the brains of a rabbit.

Foxes it is said will never pass iron. To protect their poultry, Dartmoor farmers near Poundsgate placed old barrel rings on the ground around the hen-coops, and old pieces of iron near to the roosting place of their prize hens. They claimed never to have lost a bird to a fox.

Somerset folk advise that a hen found mauled by a fox is not one to make a meal of. The teeth of the predator are thought to be poisonous, and would have infected the fowl.

A note for those living in town. Should you ever look from your window and see a fox being hunted through the streets, make sure that your insurance policy is paid up. The fox, so seen, is believed to be the precursor of a fire on the premises of the one who beholds its predicament.

Don't ever be disturbed if a moth hovers around you; it is probably flitting your way to bring the information that good news is on its way or that a letter will be delivered to you soon.

In the West Country the dragonfly has been accorded differing names in various areas such as horse longcripple, horse viper or horse adder. People often regard the dragonfly with dread and are afraid of it though it is perfectly innocuous, except to the other insects upon which it preys. The sting of the large black and yellow dragonfly is, however, deadly to horses.

When picking mushrooms in Gloucestershire, ensure that one is left for the little people, if you don't wish to feel the wrath of the Stroud pixies or Randwick fairies.

Boiled in milk with white lily roots and linseed, mushrooms produce a pulp that can be applied as a poultice to boils and abscesses. This was better than any other preparation that can be made according to Culpeper. People are more nervous about eating mushrooms than any other wild food so it is common sense, not custom, which advises that the true identity of any mushroom gathered should be double checked before a meal of them is consumed.

Those cunning creatures, rats, may not be over-welcome in many homes but in Appledore and some other sea-faring communities far from it being a matter of the rodent removing itself and sinking ships being deserted, there were times when the presence of rats was most desirable and virtually a necessity. It was considered unlucky to go to sea in a ship that had no rats aboard.

If a Shaftesbury shrew runs over your foot, it is said that you will suffer an accident that will make you lame and you will walk with a limp for the remainder of your life. There is evidence, however, to suggest that it isn't necessary to suffer them underfoot, or near your feet, at all.

A report in the *Western Morning News* of 13 February 1962 confirms that animal charming has not been lost in this century. During the winter of '62 the Three Fords Inn at Clyst St Mary was overrun with shrews. Not being a particularly unpleasant creature, the furry intruders were almost regarded as pets by the innkeeper and customers. However, sharing their home with a tribe of furry friends was not apparently a long-term prospect considered with enthusiasm by the licensee's wife. At the beginning of February she very politely asked the little creatures to leave. They did.

In the West Country areas where Britain's only venomous snake, the adder or viper, is still to be found, snakes are treated with full respect and avoided whenever possible. Adders were believed to obtain their poison by eating

Arum maculatum, wild arum. Children in Hatherleigh and many other parts of Devon were forbidden by their parents to pick wild arum - 'adder food' as it was known. North Tawton children went in fear of it as 'adder meat'.

A man named Kelland who knew of the 'old ways' lived between Yealmpton and Plympton at the beginning of this century and was known as the man who could control snakes. He perpetuated his fame when called upon by drawing a circle on the ground around a snake with a walking stick. Some say any stick would do so long as it was from an ash tree. Whatever wood it was he used, there is agreement by those who witnessed the wonder that as soon as the snake was enclosed by the mystical marks of the circle drawn by the man, the creature was unable to move out of it, and could easily be killed. Kelland the snake-charmer increased his reputation across the county when it became widely known that he could cure toothache, at a distance, without contact with the sufferer.

Snake-cracking was once a recognised sport on Dartmoor. An adder, taken by its tail, had to be cracked like a whip, quickly, to break its back. If this wasn't done quickly enough the cracker was likely to be bitten.

In Somerset it was believed that, no matter how hard you tried to kill it, a snake would not die before sunset, so snake-cracking never seemed to have caught on in the county.

The viper is still feared in Devon where it was usual to keep an addled egg at hand, the nauseous contents of which were to be swallowed as soon as possible after suffering a viper's bite.

A black toad makes a useful present when moving to another house and garden; its presence ensures good luck and fine crops.

Not so lucky for pests however: the toad you've received as a gift can be put in your cucumber frames for a time to eat up the intruders.

The 'schrudle-crub' or fieldmouse of the fruitful fields of Devon is one of nature's cuddly creatures when depicted clinging to corn-ears in calendars and cards. To the workers who might easily cross its path, the fieldmouse was regarded as a loathsome creature that, if it ran across any part of a man or a beast, would spread disease as a consequence of its lightest touch. If by chance such an encounter should happen to you, take the first feather you find lying upon the ground, from any bird, and immediately plant it with the quill end stuck firmly into the earth and the feathery portion upright. Anyone who finds this feather is guaranteed good luck according to Cotswold lore.

MEGALOMANIA ON THE MOORS

Early in the twentieth century, when mole skins were still in demand, mole trapping was a thriving business which could provide a useful income to country folk. Older, experienced trappers would draw the attention of the younger ones to the forefeet of these little animals. No matter from what depth of dirt the animal was plucked, its feet were always clean and the trappers told a tale of an arrogant lady who once lived in Devon.

On the northern edge of the moor there lived a lady who was so vain that she expected continual compliments on her beauty (which she didn't possess) and people to bow before her great knowledge (she couldn't spell and could hardly read). She was so arrogant that she lost her friends but her servants and local traders still had to put up with her ways. With little to do except make other people's lives a misery, her sole objective in life was to possess ever more beautiful clothes and adornments for her person, to enable her to show off. Spinners of wool laboured long and hard to spin fine yarn and cowered before her as she fingered it at arm's length before cursing them soundly and calling for her servants to throw them and their 'coarse' materials into the street. Her anger was unfounded, her comments caustic. She refused to pay for their hard work, so the families of the spinners went without food while the spinning wheels whirred again and more wool was spun and spun, over and over, into ever finer yarn; and the fingers of the spinners cracked with sores.

The sewing mistresses sewed fine fabrics and sorely tried their eyes by sewing only the tiniest stitches. The arrogant lady rejected their finest work of course and made them sew more, again and again, sewing until their fingers curled and froze in pain.

Lacemakers criss-crossed their pattern pins creating convoluted cobwebs that crippled their wrists, and still the fine lady demanded more: "How can one so beautiful as I use lace that is fit only to be used by fishermen?"

The plight of the lacemakers, the seamstresses, the spinners, and many more good folk who crossed the path of the moorland megalomaniac did not, however, go unnoticed. The little people, whose ancestors populated this peninsula long before any human foot trod to the end of land, listened to the thoughts of those who could not put their wishes into words. The woman, they agreed, needs bringing down to earth! Then, the little people, fairies, pixies, call them what you will, intervened.

For the suffering that she caused to others because of her pride, the little people turned her into a mole, condemned forever to burrow through the darkness of the earth. To remind her of the harm she had caused to others and the life she had wasted, her own, the little people clothed her in a fur that never was to be stained or soiled by the earth through which she dug. To remind us all that it is by our own hand that we shape our future, the little people provided her with the softest paws of any cold-earth creature.

5 Weather or Not

The weather in the West Country can change very quickly in some places. On Bodmin Moor, Dartmoor or Exmoor some say that it is possible to experience the weather of all seasons in a single day and people living in the coastal areas make similar claims. While they may all be exaggerating, if only slightly, as far as the West Country weather is concerned, knowing which way the wind is blowing, so to speak, can't be a bad thing.

Associating the presence, or habits, of all kind of creatures with the weather is as widespread throughout the West Country as anywhere else, and some sayings or rhymes contain some good advice.

Better weather should be the order of the day by the time the cuckoo arrives in April but:

When the cuckoo sits on an empty bough
Keep your hay and sell your cow.

No leaves on trees, a late spring and little food for cattle left from over-winter stocks become all too clear a warning that summer is a long way off.

That summer weather is important to many people in the West Country such as the holiday visitors, the farmers and the fishermen, who all look for 'the signs'. The long-term forecast gained from observing the oak and ash is well known enough, so we won't repeat it here. Instead, consider the moon as a monthly forecaster:

A Saturday moon, and a Sunday Full,
Ne'er did good, and ne'er w'll.
A Saturday's change to a Sunday's Full,
Comes too soon, whene'er it w'll.

When the full moon arrives on a Sunday, the weather in the following month can be expected to be bad both on land and at sea. The new moon can make or mar the days ahead:

Upright new moon
Good weather soon.
The new moon's lying on her back
Watching the clouds in the sky turn black.

Whichever you see, don't forget to turn your money over in your pocket or purse for good luck, but don't look at the new moon through the window while you're doing it.

More down to earth forecasting is a cock crowing near the house, forecasting good weather; a braying donkey will also do. Holiday-makers probably won't have brought their cat with them but if they see a local one washing its face, 'over its ear', the skies above will be bright and clear. If, however, the cat is seen screeching down the road, and taking the corner on two paws, the signs are not too good. That cat obviously has a storm tied to its tail.

Check that probability out by seeking some rooks, and if they are flying low, our best suggestion is that the time has come for you to look for some indoor entertainment for all the family. If there happens to be a thunderstorm, spare a thought for the people of Ludgan in Cornwall who, it is said, opened their doors during a thunderstorm to let the lightning enter their house and bring good fortune to them.

When Somerset folk see the blackthorn bearing blossom, they don't expect to see good weather again for a week or two.

After a summer storm in Cornwall the rainbow isn't just a pretty sight:

See a rainbow in the morn, take a hook and cut the corn.
See a rainbow in the eve, put your hook into the sheave.

The forecast is clear: get working as the weather betters, or get the cut corn in before it worsens. The fishermen can also benefit from reading the rainbow:

Rainbow to windward, foul falls the day.
Rainbow to leeward, rain clears away.

The consequence of a red sky, at night or in the morning, is known well enough, but advice gained from a mackerel sky is just as useful:

A mackerel sky forming
Twelve hour 'til storm warning.

While taking a stroll around Gloucestershire's lanes, the poor man's weather-vane, the scarlet pimpernel, will advise you whether or not to continue your walk. If the flower is open, a dry spell will be enjoyed; if the flower is closed, then rain is due:

Pimpernell, Pimpernell, tell me so,
If tomorrow's weather be fine, or no;
My heart can't feel, my tongue can't tell
But you know true sweet Pimpernell.

During the summer, low-flying swallows are a sure sign of rain while when they fly high they foretell a clear sky. Devon poet and playwright John Gay, in his first 'Pastoral', wrote:

When swallows fleet soar high and sport in air,
He told us that the welkin would be clear.

But an old summer saying advises that:

If the cockerel crows on going to bed,
He's bound to arise with rain overhead.

A dry May and a dripping June

Leaves August damp and September out of tune.

October's frosts in Devon could be relied upon to be good indicators of the winter weather that would follow on:

Ice in October to bear up a duck,
Winter to follow with slush and muck.

Further inland, ducks in Somerset and Wiltshire were not approved forecasters of the approaching winter's weather until they were seen, on ice, in November but there were opportunities for others to make their feelings known:

> When the hen doth moult afore th' cock,
> Winter coming will be hard as rock.
> A moulting cock 'fore a moulting hen,
> Winter coming 'll be dry again.

Deep in the Devon countryside in the week leading up to December the appearance of seagulls could cast gloom across hopes of a mild winter in the coming new year and an old rhyme explained the reason:

> Sea-gull, sea-gull stay by the sand.
> Thee'll bring nought but bad weather
> If thee flies far inland.

The arrival of winter didn't stop the forecasters:

> A January spring
> Makes February ring.

Don't trust the weather was their cry:

> Green January
> Full churchyard.

But, if the weather wasn't spring-like, then the forecasts came in a flurry:

> Snow, staying on the ground some time, is a waiting for more t' join 'n.

And the forecasters certainly began to add advice to their predictions:

> Walk fast in snow,
> In frost walk slow,
> And still as you go,
> Tread on your toe.

> When frost and snow lie both together
> Stay by your fire and save shoe-leather.

Forecasts for farmers were not forgotten and they were warned that over-wintered stock needed their attention and feed must be preserved for there was a lot of winter still to come:

> From Christmas to May
> Weak cattle decay
> A farm must have on Candlemas Day
> Half its straw and half its hay.

In March it is advisable to count all the frogs that are seen during the month since the creatures forewarn of later weather:

> As many frogs in March . . . So many frosts in May.

The country beekeepers could always rely on their friends to warn them of inclement weather. When many bees enter a hive and none leave, it is a sign of rain approaching, and particular attention was given to the bees on Lady Day, 25 March, to see what they would say about the summer prospects:

> If the bees stay in the hive
> Summer rains they must survive.

If the bees all fly away
Summer sun will warm each day.

Not to be put off, the forecasters added their reminders:

Till April is dead
Change not a thread.
Till May is out
Cast not a clout

A Devonian verse to describe Dartmoor weather:

Fust it rain'd then it blaw'd
Then it 'ail'd then it snaw'd
Then it com'd a shower o' rain
Then it vreez'd an blaw'd agean.

Be warned! Three successive frosty mornings will bring rain. Weather lore at Woodleigh rules that:

When a saucepan boils dry, it is going to rain.

The Devon version of a rhyme about the three April days lost to March can also give useful weather guidance:

March borru'd from April three rare days
T'elp the seasons settle their ways
If on the first the rain doth fall
A summer wet us'll befall
If on the second winds do blow
Autumn gales will come enow
If on the third snow lays behind
Fear naught a winter-time unkind.

For the observant West Country visitor or resident, there is local advice that can certainly be followed, to advantage quite often:

Straight up to the sky, skylarks rising
Good weather coming, over the horizon.

When the black-back snails cross your path
The darkening clouds much moisture hath.

A frog on the hill
Brings water to the mill.

When Kits Hill monument is plainly seen
There'll be heavy rain by early e'en.

We found similar advice offered throughout the West Country so, if you don't happen to be in Cornwall and looking at Kits Hill, do feel free to change the name to a similarly prominent and well-known local landmark near you. The result is likely to be exactly the same.

The brightness in the green grass of the West Country is possibly explained most clearly in the little Dorset rhyme:

The South winds always bring us wet weather;
The North wind brings us both wet and cold, together

The West wind always brings us rain
And the East wind blows 'em all back to us again.

The first day of the first month could be relied upon to foretell the winter's tale for weather:

If January Kalends come bright and gay
Winter's weather will stay till the Kalends of May.

Perhaps the one to watch out for though, and even hope for, must be the one promising a short winter that can leave everyone looking forward to a true, long West Country summer:

If Candlemas Day passes fair and fine,
Only half the winter is left behind
But if Candlemas Day do bluster and blow
Then winter is over, as all good folk know.

6 Grave Matters

Nan Tow's Tump at Didmarten is accorded by tradition as the burial place of the Cotswold witch of that name who is said to have been buried there standing upright.

Rosemary, a symbol of constancy, is sometimes wrapped in white linen and placed upon a coffin at a funeral.

A single snowdrop is regarded as a token of death, as it is said to resemble a corpse in its shroud. The flower bears the blame for all deaths in February.

A Cotswold custom requires that numbers should not be used when a corpse is measured for a coffin. A single length of string is to be used into which three knots are to be tied: one for the length of the body; one for the body width at the shoulders; one for the body width at the hips. The string is used but once, and then destroyed.

Deaths occurring "a-tween the old Christmas and the new" in some Dorset villages were considered to be a forecast of others to come. If there were deaths in a village between 25 December and 6 January, the new Christmas and the old one, then it was believed that there would be a great many more deaths in the area during the coming year. Writing in the Dorset *County Chronicles* for March 1889, Miss Summers said that she knew of a death occuring in the village at Hazlebury Bryan during these dates that winter and, at the time of writing, she was already aware of nine funerals having followed in its wake.

Not too long ago, a funeral took place one cold, wet February morning in a South Hams church. The moorland mist, creeping around a tor and sweeping down the valley to the churchyard, drifted across the mourners arriving in pairs at the wooden gates of the granite block church on the fifteenth day of that month.

One elderly mourner, a cousin of the deceased, glanced across the groups of people that had gathered to pay their last respects. A flicker of concern crossed her brow. Something was wrong, perhaps dreadfully wrong.

The lady pulled her coat collar close to her chin and looked past people she knew and peered through the soft, greyish mist that lurked in the empty lane. To any who observed her searching gaze she was, quite obviously, a worried woman.

Her own daughter had noted the concern and her mother's eyes darting to and fro across those lamenting the loss of a loved one. She was aware of the continual glances her mother made up and down the tree-lined lane where gaunt guards stood silently waiting for winter's passing and the return of buds to their branches.

"Mother," she muttered, more towards the ground than in the direction of the lady in question. "What's the matter with you?"

Hardly distracted by the question, the woman collapsed further into her coat but continued her quest as she ignored her daughter and moved away to a better observation point. There was still no sign of anyone else coming down the lane and, trying not to be observed in her actions, she counted the assembled figures for the sixth or seventh time. Her daughter caught up with her, ushering her own offspring around their grandmother as the funeral director tactfully indicated for all those gathered to follow the coffin and the immediate family into the church.

"There are thirty-seven people here," the woman said as her daughter caught her by the arm and guided her forward. "And you can let go of my arm. I can manage, thank you."

"What are you fussing about, Mother ?"

The line of mourners moved respectfully forward.

"Thirty-seven people,"was the reply. "One of the children should have been left at home," she continued. "There'll be another of us ready for our grave within a year, you mark my words."

"Mother," exclaimed her exasperated daughter. "Don't you go a-filling the children's heads with such nonsense."

As they approached the porch she gathered her brood around her and marshalled them into the church, hard on the heels of their grandmother.

"You mark my words my girl," muttered the old lady as the three generations took their seats in a pew. "There'll be another gathering of the family around a grave before a year has gone by."

"Do be quiet Mother. Let Aunt Grace go in peace, and get your glasses out ready."

The elderly lady fumbled in her handbag for her spectacles as her youngest grandchild, in spite of her eleven years, cuddled up to her own mother for comfort.

"Don't you take any notice of that silly old granny of yours," the child's mother whispered as she tried to open her hymn book with one hand while using the other to stroke the girl's hair.

The service, the burial and the ceremonial feasting passed all too slowly for them all. That traditional solemn salute to the deceased, the consumption of quartered sandwiches, tiny sausage rolls and massed mixtures of cake, did nothing to remove the old lady's concern that an unequal number of mourners had been present on the sad occasion.

"Talk about a close family. They haven't seen each other for centuries," she said to her daughter as she added sugar to her tea. "Apart from a Christmas card I don't think Grace kept in touch with any of them."

"Well, they all turned up when they were needed, Mother."

"Yes, and you watch them looking at each other when they go, all of 'em wondering whose funeral they'll meet at next. And that won't be before long, I can tell you."

The grandchild listened, and remembered.

Visiting her grandmother each Sunday, almost as a ritual, the child sometimes recalled that February funeral as she passed the church, but never did she mention it to her mother. In the springtime the hedgerows were flooded with a welcome yellow tide of primroses and their fragile beauty could still be found in secret places when the fields of bluebells began to show the way towards summertime. The child half expected to hear that some other once-met relative had passed away but the fear diminished as the campion swayed in the summer sun and the thoughts planted in bleak February were lost in the trenches of time.

The summer solstice came, and passed; autumn's equinox too.

Christmas they shared and enjoyed as a family, the new year they welcomed in the same way, then grandmother died - on St Valentine's Day.

Snow lay on the ground and the tor was shrouded in cloud as the black-overcoated bearers brought the coffin into the granite block church on another February morn. Dutifully and solemnly the children walked with their parents behind the coffin towards the candle-lit chancel. One pair of eyes had already noted that, including their own, forty-three pairs of feet would follow the bier. The concern her grandmother had known a year before, the child shared again that day. In the very prime of her life, her mother died, just before Christmas that same year.

Two generations passed away, each within the year allotted by lore.

At some Devon funerals, a count was kept on the numbers of mourners attending the service, to ensure that an equal number went through the lychgate. It was thought that the odd one out, when an unequal number passed through, was the Devil's disciple looking for someone to meet his master before the year was out. To maintain even numbers, it was not uncommon for a child to be refused admission to the funeral service.

7 The Lore of the Trees

Forests once covered the West Country and in many places the still-wooded hills and valleys can be visited to provide us with the opportunity to understand by experience that little has changed since our Celtic ancestors walked these lands two thousand years ago. Oak and elm have given way down the centuries to other trees but the magic of the forest, something words can hardly describe, exists still for those who have the will to find it.

Of all the trees that grow so fair,
Old England to adorn
Greater are none beneath the Sun,
Than Oak, and Ash, and Thorn.
England shall bide, till Judgement Tide
by Oak, and Ash, and Thorn !

Rudyard Kipling

The oak was regarded as sacred by Celtic and Scandinavian peoples and, long after the Druids gathered in groves of oak, the tree is still a magnet for many groups and individuals who regard it as magical. The oak became the symbol of England and reason was found to celebrate it that proved acceptable to the Church.

After the battle of Worcester in 1651 Charles II escaped with his life when he hid in the Boscobel Oak to avoid his Parliamentary pursuers and thus the oak tree took on an almost 'holy' aura. Across the country oak leaves were worn to commemorate the escape and in 1660 when he returned to London on his birthday, 29 May, to take up his throne again, oak leaves were worn until midday, then substituted with ash leaves until sunset. The wearing of the oak leaf on 29 May is a tradition kept alive by many people to this day.

In some Dorset and Wiltshire areas Oak Apple Day celebrations confirm the day's pagan origins. The presentation of green boughs to the Dean at the high altar of Salisbury Cathedral, the traditional cry, "Grovely! Grovely! Grovely! and all Grovely !", the traditional dance on the green outside the cathedral, bear no relevance to the escape of a king, but contain a far older significance. The relevance of the king's escape is reduced further by local celebrations that commemorate the defeat of an Earl of Wilton instead; but the celebration of the oak continues. Oak Apple Day has survived in the West Country as a day of festivity, still celebrated, if perhaps only by a few.

As a forecaster of weather the oak shares pride of place with the ash and there are many variations around the country of the Somerset rhyme already mentioned that forecasts the weather from the tree first to show leaves in spring:

If the Oak before the Ash
Then there'll only be a splash
If the Ash before the Oak
Then prepare for a mighty soak.

Oaks have been associated with all manner of festivities, marriages, deaths and gospel reading. Visitors to West Country churches might observe just how often the oak leaf, or the bough, is depicted in the carvings in stone or wood to be found on walls, pulpits or pews. Look at the gates of old houses and find the acorn, and find it also on window cords and light pulls. Observe how often the oak can still be found as the centre-tree on many a village green or meeting place.

The oak is a far from forgotten tree and is one that can dispense justice, according to a Somerset story. Among the many people condemned to death during the Bloody Assizes by the notorious Judge Jeffreys was one whose quartered body was boiled by his own friend who undertook the horrific task on the judge's order, to save himself from sentence. The man was given a new surname by all who were appalled by his callous act and it was as Boilman that the man became known.

His body was found one day beneath the branches of an oak tree. Lightning had killed him, without doubt, but it was the oak tree that was considered to have directed justice.

Robert Herrick, literary figure, oft-quoted recorder of rural life and vicar of a Devon parish wrote:

Dearest, bury me,
Under that holy oke, or Gospel Tree,
Where, though thou seest not, thou mayst
Think upon Me, when you yearly go'st procession.

The ash tree is one of the most magical trees, providing protection against witchcraft, curing ills, detailing the future through divination and acting as a weather guide.

A Dorset girl, not long ago, would take an ash leaf and divine who her future husband would be. She would be pluck an ash leaf from the tree and, holding it in her hand, she would say:

"The even ash leaf in my hand,
The first I meet shall be my man."

Then she put the leaf in her glove and said:

"The even ash leaf in my glove,
The first man I meet shall be my true love."

Then, with leaf transferred to her bosom:

"The even ash leaf in my bosom,
The true love I meet shall my husband be.

It is a leaf that is said to bring good luck to anyone fortunate enough to find one growing:

Even ash leaf as I thee pluck
Into my life deliver luck.

The use of ash twigs by water diviners, instead of hazel, is not unknown in Dorset or in Gloucestershire but in Devon the ash had, and has, particular uses.

In the 1600s wise people out walking looked upon the leaves of the ash tree as a reliable charm against the bites of snakes and always carried some with them.

It is recorded by many, including Pliny, that to trace a circle with an ash stick around a sleeping snake is enough to kill the creature. A variation of this we found in Somerset where a Brewham man related how, when he was a boy, he had been taught to catch snakes with a long-handled, forked ash stick. The snake, pinned behind the head with forked ash, went rigid, he claimed, which rendered it safe and easy to handle.

However, if a snake is disturbed, and it strikes at and bites the person doing the tracing or pinning, they may be comforted to know of a snake-bite remedy we were advised by a countryman living near Plymouth. He suggested that a circle of ash twigs placed around the neck of the victim would ensure an adequate cure.

An adder, it is said, will die instantly if struck a clear, clean, single blow - but beware. Death will only result if the blow is delivered using a weapon made from ash wood. However, adders only attack if provoked so are best left alone.

There is one traditional anti-snake precaution that can be employed by those who might wish to walk where such snakes dwell. Understanding its protective values, they might consider it wise to purchase an ash walking stick. These, not surprisingly perhaps, are available in country areas where snakes may be encountered.

The ash tree was, and still is, used in many ways. For centuries, at Christmas time or New Year, the ashen faggot was burned in every hearth. People in different areas of the West Country followed tradition on differing dates, some on Christmas Eve, some when seeing the old year out.

Ash branches, perhaps a dozen but sometimes more, some as thick as an arm, others thin, and all determined in length only by the size of a fireplace, were bound together by thin strips of the tree itself, or with withy (willow) or hazel. The bonds, in groups of three, varied in number, nine or fifteen being the most often used. Families, friends, workers, guests, all coming together for the festivity in a private house or public inn were provided with free food and liquid refreshment. With due ceremony the ashen 'faggot' was laid on the fire and when each bond burst among the flames the glasses of the assembled company were filled again, and again, and again, as words written by J Thorn in 1795 confirm:

The ponderous ashen faggot, from the yard
The farmer to his crowded hall conveys, with speed;
Where, on the rising flames
Already fed with store of massy brands, it blazes soon;
Nine bandages it bears and as they each disjoin, as custom wills,
A mighty jug of sparkling cyder's brought
With brandy mix'd, to elevate the guests.

When the faggot is about to be placed upon the fire, unmarried maidens each choose one of the bands and wait for their selected band to burst in the heat. The girl whose band breaks first can be sure to marry before her friends.

This traditional burning survives in many a farmhouse today where the old fireplaces permit a sizeable ashen faggot to be used when friends and family are freely entertained. Some inns, with more suitable-sized ashen faggots used, have maintained the custom or revived it.

In 1992, when the then new landlord of the Devonshire Inn at Sticklepath near Okehampton decided to revive the tradition of burning the ashen faggot in the fire of the bar, the faggot burned with an increasing amount of smoke which filled the bar and virtually the entire pub, forcing smiling regulars out on to the village street. They were smiling because each forced exit provided them with another drink, courtesy of mine host, the courtesy of a very soot-covered, smoke-ridden, host it would be fair to say but it was a host who was not to be deterred and who persevered until the faggot flared. Fortunately for tradition, the landlord's attempt to revive the custom found favour with everyone. Christmas visitors will still find the ashen faggot being fired at the Devonshire Inn - but with less smoke and more flair, perhaps.

In woodburning areas the ash tree has a practical value like none other: it burns while still green and can be cut and used virtually at once.

At the time of Saturnalia, the forerunner of Christmas, branches of bay were the favoured decoration of the Romans. It was the tree they associated with honour, fame and victory. It was also a great protector and healer.

Every part of the bay tree, sacred to Apollo and Aesculapius, god of medicine, was used in the West Country to concoct a remedy for some complaint or other and the tree is a living medical cabinet of cures. The bark or the root is used to treat gall and kidney stones, open the 'innards' and to relieve obstructions. The berries provide an antidote to wasp and bee stings, and all poisons of venomous creatures, and are used against pestilence and infectious diseases. According to Culpeper, the berries "mightily expel the wind, provoke urine, help the mother, and kill the worms". The leaves, dried and mixed with honey or syrup, provide protection against the Plague and can help the brain, eyes, lungs and many other parts of the body.

The bay is one of the best trees to have near the home since, besides its medical values, it will never be struck by lightning. If a bay tree withers and dies however this can only be viewed as a sign of impending disaster for the household. In Shakespeare's *Richard III*, the Welsh captain departs from the presence of the Earl of Salisbury, saying:

> It is thought the King is dead; we will not stay.
> The bay-trees in our country are all withered,
> And meteors fright the fixed stars of heaven.

The sounds made by bay leaves could speak of the future it was said. When they are thrown on a fire, crackling leaves forecast that good fortune is coming your way; but quiet, smouldering leaves tell you that ill luck is near.

On St Valentine's Day, a young Cornish maid gains an insight into the future by sprinkling bay leaves with water and laying them upon her pillow in the evening. Later, when she retires to bed, she must dress in a clean nightgown and repeat these words before going to sleep:

Good Valentine be kind to me
In dreams let me my true love see.

He will, and she will.

West Country lovers pick a laurel (sweet bay) twig; each then breaks their twig in two and, with a promise to be true, exchanges one half with the other, so each retains two halves, one pair. From that time on each must maintain, undivided, their twinned laurel twigs and, while they do, no broken promises will harm their hearts, their love will flourish, and never shall they part. Laurel leaves burned on a fire are helpful in encouraging the return of a straying loved one.

In many West Country areas the blossom of the spiky blackthorn was feared more than the blossom of the may tree, though both threatened to bring disaster if brought into a house.

Blackthorn, with its reputation as an omen of death, was banned from being taken indoors in many counties throughout the UK and such traditions continue despite a modern generation often mocking the beliefs of their 'superstitious' parents.

Like the Glastonbury Thorn (a hawthorn tree), blackthorn is said to bloom at midnight on Old Christmas Eve and is reputed to be the tree from which Christ's crown of thorns was made. Even as a tree feared by many, the blackthorn can be found at times used in Christmas decorations, taking its place alongside the Druidic mistletoe, but when it is used it is first scorched and burned by fire.

Paying penance for its use as a crown provides Christian connotations to the blackthorn but its past use in pagan fire festivities is traditionally continued in areas where branches of blackthorn are burned and the ashes scattered on the land to ensure crop fertility.

In Dorset, newly-grown thorns known as 'maidenthorns' were picked and stuck into the heart of a horse or some other animal, as charms against witchcraft. The thorn- and pin-pierced hearts of horses, bullocks, oxen or cows were placed by custom in a chimney or in the roof of a building before it was completed, to give protection. The chimney was important, since, unlike a door or window, it could never be closed and always afforded the witch an easy way in. Pins were sometimes used instead of thorns and a cottage being renovated near Exeter provided one example of this practice when a dried-out, pin-pricked heart was found.

Examples of the use of the blackthorn have been discovered in other parts of the West Country also.

Once one of the mightiest trees to be found in England, the elm has largely been lost recently to Dutch elm disease. Traditionally it was believed that lightning would not strike an elm and it was used in many areas to make maypoles. The long association of the elm with fairy folk gave the tree the country name of elven. To show the little people where human rule held sway the customary 'beating of the bounds' in many counties included the use of an elm branch to literally 'beat' points around the boundary to make sure the elves were aware that humans would not intrude into their domain.

It is considered unlucky throughout the Western counties to bring may (hawthorn blossom) into the home. Whoever brings hawthorn into the house will bring sickness to a family member.

Simply to sit under a hawthorn tree in Cornwall or Devon is extremely dangerous. It challenges the pixies to put a spell upon you and take you into their power.

The dew taken by a Somerset maiden from hawthorn blossom on a May morning was used as a beauty treatment; Samuel Pepys recorded that his wife bathed in it, as an aid to beauty.

In the Cotswolds, the tree was believed to possess magical qualities and protective powers and was prominently displayed on cottages and houses to keep them free from evil, repel witches, ghosts and spirits, and safeguard the property against storms.

The old country custom of fastening hawthorn up outside cowsheds on May Day (1 May) was explained in Camborne as being a means of providing protection for the cows from the pixies or witches who steal their milk, while outside Truro the reason given was that it would ensure the cows gave a good milk flow during the coming year.

A hawthorn branch was recently seen securely attached to a cowshed near Warmister but the farmer said he knew nothing about it. Four months later the branch was still there. The following year it was replaced by a new fresh green one, just as securely attached as its predecessor.

The pagan 'Green Man' symbol (a pagan representation of the spirit of summer or of fertility) wears a hawthorn wreath to represent pleasure at the return of summer. The symbol can still be seen in medieval churches, or inn signs, where it is sometimes in the guise of 'Jack in the Green' or 'Robin Hood'.

The Glastonbury Thorn is a hawthorn tree said to have grown from the staff of St Joseph of Arimathea when he stuck it into the ground of Wearyall Hill, Glastonbury. It took root immediately and burst into leaf.

In January 1753 the *Gentleman's Magazine* noted that a great many people went to see the Thorn on Christmas Day but there was no sign of it 'blowing' (blooming). They returned again in January when it was seen to bloom as usual, on Old Christmas Day.

This was taken as a clear indication of the error in using the new calendar and that the old calendar was still correct.

Hazel is another tree with magical powers and it is still used by water diviners who use a forked branch to locate water. The divining rod acts best if cut on St John's Eve, or night, 23/24 June. In addition to showing where water is to be found, until the sixteenth century the hazel rod was used to detect thieves. When pointed at a group of people suspected of villainy the rod twitched as it was carried towards them and almost tore itself from the hands of the user whenever it came close to the offender.

To the Celts two thousand years ago the tree was associated with fire and fertility. To later peoples the hazel had many uses, for both humans and animals. Leaves eaten by cows would increase their milk yield. Adder bites could be healed by laying a cross of hazel twigs across the wound. A double hazelnut carried in the pocket prevented toothache. Placing a hazel breast-band on a horse protected it from the fairies.

Young ladies in Gloucestershire were warned against going nutting, because it could endanger their maidenhood. Devon maids made good use of hazelnuts on Hallowe'en. A row of nuts was placed among the embers of a fire on St Mark's Eve (24 April), each named for one girl present. The names of suitors were spoken and, if a girl's nut popped when her suitor's name was heard, it was a sign that his suit would succeed:

If you love me, pop and fly.
If not, lie and die.

For most of us, our annual connection with the holly tree is when its red-berried sprigs are with merry anticipation borne into the home. But beware. According to Devon custom, to take holly into the house before Christmas is to invite ill fortune in with it. It is also considered very unlucky to burn holly, and good fortune, says the old custom, will not favour those who keep holly in the house after 6 January, Old Christmas Day.

The holly has been a sacred tree since pre-Christian times and some Christians regard it with suspicion. Most congregations however include holly among their church decorations and often, surprisingly perhaps, retain their decorations beyond 6 January.

The proper time for removing the holly and evergreens after Christmas used to be after Candlemas was celebrated on 2 February.

When the decorations were eventually removed from castle, church or cottage, every last scrap of greenery had to be taken:

That so the superstitious find,
Not one least branch there left behind,
For look, how many leaves there be,
Neglected there, maids trust to me,
So many goblins you shall see.

One of the safest places to be in a thunderstorm is said to be beneath a holly tree. Lightning is supposed never to strike holly.

In the mid-1950s, two prominent holly trees were cut down in Chittlehampton, bringing violent protests from some local residents who believed that this act of folly would produce poltergeist havoc.

If the fruit of the holly tree appears in profusion it will be a severe winter as the plentiful supply of berries is said to be there to provide food for the birds.

Whatever their opinion of holly, the early Christians certainly objected to the use of ivy, because of its Bacchanalian association, but the usefulness of the plant ensured its long connection with cures and divination.

If it grew on a house the place was safe from witches but if it withered and died so would the fortunes of those living within.

On New Year's Eve an ivy leaf was placed on a dish of water and left until Twelfth Night; if then it was still green and fresh the coming year would bring good fortune.

Black spots appearing in the middle of the leaf were a warning of stomach troubles; at the pointed end the spots warned of problems arising with feet and legs; and near the stalk the attention would be drawn to troubles with the neck and head.

If the leaf had decayed by Twelfth Night, the person consulting it should prepare for their own death.

A vinegar of ivy berries was a popular remedy during and after the time of the Great Plague of 1665. Water and wine mixed in an ivy-wood bowl are said to separate; ivy leaves and berries have been used in potions found to be helpful after a bout of heavy drinking.

Not a tree, but certainly of it, mistletoe is perhaps the foremost mystical or mysterious plant.

Its significance has endured for thousands of years since the Druids used it at the winter and summer solstice celebrations. The popular present-day custom of kissing beneath a sprig is possibly an echo, down through the centuries, of its earlier sexual significance which led it to being banned from churches. A traditional garland for 'Jack in the Green', the ritual figure that heralds the coming of summer, mistletoe has been revered and used in ceremonial for centuries.

Hung on doorways it offers protection to a home and inhabitants while also being a visible sign of peace and hospitality. A sprig, laid in a cradle, keeps the baby safe from pixies.

Mistletoe is mystically declared the poison of the apple tree, coming up from the roots, but fruit farmers often suggest that apple trees growing close together will not do well unless there is mistletoe growing on them somewhere.

Generally, any of it used during the festive season is taken down along with all the other Christmas decorations, around about the time of Twelfth Night, but there are exceptions. It is a long-established West Country belief that a piece should remain in place throughout the year. Around Chudleigh we were advised that mistletoe left hanging in the home from one Christmas to the next will protect the premises from being struck by lightning. In Cheltenham people told us that to observe the tradition of keeping mistletoe in the home all year round would ensure that the residents will never go hungry or be without bread.

In all the West Country counties we found confirmation that the rowan tree provided protection against witches and evil-doers. Even those who professed no personal belief confessed knowledge of such things, often gained in childhood.

In times when wood was used to fashion most tools used in a farm dairy, a rowan twig in the churn, or a churn staff of rowan, kept the butter safe from evil interference. A piece of rowan in a person's pocket kept them safe from the evil eye, or being 'overlooked'. Carters used rowan whips so that their horses would not be bewitched.

In Dorset and on down through Cornwall, the recognition and respect for the rowan, its values and its many magical properties, particularly those relating to protection, appear to have increased in recent years. Perhaps this is one reason the tree has become so popular in gardens today.

Crosses made from rowan are regarded as great protectors only if the wood used has been broken from the tree. The wood must not be cut with a metal saw, or a knife or any implement - only the hand can be used - and the tree must be 'asked' to provide its power.

"Plant your pears, for your heirs" is a widely-used saying. The pear tree was such a slow-growing tree that it was not favoured by fruit growers except in areas where perry was made as an alternative to cider. In some West Country districts however there are many who claim that the pear holds great powers of protection, and that it is a stronger charm against evil even than the rowan. A token or talisman made from pear tree wood provides the most reliable protection against witches. A love spoon or loving cup fashioned from pear wood will ensure life-long fidelity between the partners, who exchange them as gifts, and the cradle made from pear wood will ensure that the babe within grows to be honest, true, faithful and reliable.

The yew, known to live long itself, is widely recognised as a symbol of long life. Relic boxes, and weapons, including crossbows were made from it. Curious blends of pagan ritual and Christian tradition are retained in Gloucestershire, Hereford and Worcester, where the yew tree in the churchyard becomes a centre-piece for celebration with people dancing round it.

It is also a tree popularly used to decorate churches where, in some cases, it is used at Whitsuntide and the branches retained in the church till the following year.

The yew tree at Stoke Gabriel is said to grant your wish if you walk around it, backwards, seven times.

A staff cut from a yew tree will help a walker pass many a mile with ease, and a wand pulled, not cut, from the yew will ward off any attack by witches and keep a sleeper safe at night if left by the bedroom door.

8 Country Cures and Rural Remedies

The late-twentieth-century 'New Age' has produced alternatives to just about everything, including medicine but, in the gardens of Devon, country cures and rural remedies have abounded for centuries.

A south Devon charm widely used to cure boils, or blackheads as they are known locally, calls for a horseshoe nail and a piece of elder twig two inches long and three-eighths of an inch in diameter. The horseshoe nail is forced down through the pith of the elder until the head projects at one end and the point protrudes at the other. If, in forcing the nail through the twig, the twig splits, start again with another twig. When it is successfully protruding from the twig the point of the nail should be cut off, leaving the nail enclosed in elder. The amulet, for this is what is has now become, must then be wrapped tightly in clean linen tape and the whole thing sewn into a close-fitting linen pouch. Remember which end of the amulet holds the nail head and to that end attach a piece of narrow tape, exactly thirteen inches long, to form a loop for the neck. The charm is now ready to be worn by the person suffering from blackheads who must keep it around their neck at all times until they are cured.

Alternatively, it is suggested that for early risers the removal of boils can be achieved by crawling backwards round a thorn bush three times, at sunrise, while the dew is on the ground.

Ringmore residents insist that all that is required to remove boils is for the sufferer to obtain a nutmeg from a member of the opposite sex. The nutmeg, kept in the pocket or purse, must be nibbled occasionally and by the time the nutmeg has been consumed the boil will have gone.

Losing a boil is something to be desired; to lose one's hair is not. As menfolk got older there were country cures to prevent baldness. A comb made from rosemary wood and used daily would stimulate hair growth, or a wreath of ivy worn regularly would stop the hair from falling out. If, however, these rural remedies failed for some reason it was almost certain that a witch was at work - a witch who needed human hair to weave into her or his - spells. The known way to defeat the witch, while also protecting the head, was for the hair loss sufferer to obtain water from deep hollows around beech trees. The water was carried home to be boiled in a pot on the open fire with lots of rosemary added to the pan. The elixir produced would stop hair loss and prevent baldness but, if it didn't work, a compound obtained from the crushed roots of Solomon's seal was a guaranteed cure for baldness. Inhaling the brewed flowers of Solomon's seal induced inspiration.

At the other extreme, corns can be cured by using a popular cottage garden recipe relied upon at Rattery. Collect a basketful of ivy leaves at midday, preferably from a location where the sun has been shining on the leaves all morning, and place them in saucepan with some rainwater and vinegar. Bring the mixture to the boil and then allow it to simmer for thirty minutes. Strain the ivy leaf pulp and make a poultice, which can then be bound around the corns as a reliable remedy.

To ensure a peaceful night's sleep free from cramp according to a lady from Loddiswell, place your stockings, or socks, crosswise on the bottom of your bed when retiring. If this fails there was a long-term remedy that required some preparation. It is first necessary to acquire some used coffin nails. These, of necessity, must be retrieved from a grave and are reputed to be a guaranteed cramp cure, when made into a ring which is then worn at all times on the middle finger of the left hand.

Other nails, those on fingers or toes, could contribute to health and happiness.

Cut your nails on Monday and you cut them for health
Cut your nails on Tuesday and you cut them for wealth
Cut your nails on Wednesday and you cut them for luck
Cut your nails on Thursday, no luck at all
Cut your nails on Friday, you're sure to fall
Cut your nails on Saturday, the best day of all,
and in the workhouse you won't go
On Sunday you don't cut your nails at all.

Variations on the advice generally suggested that Friday was always an unlucky day for nail cutting, to cut nails on a Saturday ensured that lovers would meet next day but, for any who dared cut them on a Sunday, their punishment would be to have the Devil sit on their shoulder all through the week.

Who on the Sabbath pares his horn
Twere better for him had he never been born.

Times change and cures come and go. For many years a soldier could provide a cure when called upon and shot, used in muskets, could be coated in butter and given to children to swallow as a cure for croup. In swallowing the shot the passage of the throat would be cleared.

A successful remedy for itching is told of in Totnes, but is suspected as being one known and recommended with enthusiasm by mischievous mariners from downstream Dartmouth. The recipe, as related, required that you: "Mix together one quarter of a pound of lard with two ounces of gunpowder; make a salve from this compound and rub it all over the parts what itches." It was also recommended that the patient, once having received the treatment, should sit near the fire! The actual efficacy of the cure, which should not be doubted, depends, probably, on a slight variation to the advice given to itch sufferers by a gun crew known to have served with Nelson at Trafalgar. While the recipe remained the same the added advice provided to friends was that, once the salve has been applied, the patient should 'not' sit near the fire.

For the treatment of scrofula, a probable tubercular condition affecting the lymphatic glands also known as the 'king's evil', cure is assured if the patient can procure the use of a 'dead hand'. Reginald Scot, writing in his

Discoverie of Witchcraft in 1584 left us some admirable advice when he affirmed that: "To heal the king's or queen's evil, or any other soreness of the throat, first touch the place with the hand of one that died an untimely death."

In a more general application of the principle, Hunt in his *Popular Romances of the West of England* says that "Placing the hand of a man, who died by his own act, is a cure for many diseases." He went on to record the cure of young man who had been afflicted with running tumours since his birth and also said that he, "once saw a young woman led on to the scaffold, in the Old Bailey, for the purpose of having a wen [a benign tumour on the skin, particularly the scalp] touched with the hand of a man who had just been executed."

There has always been a touch of humour to some of the rural remedies and sayings:

It wasn't the cough that carried him off
It was the coffin they carried him off in.

But in Dartmouth, it was a boat, that was set afloat, to cure the cough, that saw victims off.

One of the rural remedies for whooping cough was to take the patient 'twice over water', by taking a boat across a river and back again, but for those who couldn't afford this the alternative was to sit the patient, usually a child, on the bank of a river estuary, with its back to water while the tide came in and went back out again. If that didn't achieve the desired result there was a remedy prescribed by a well-known wise woman on Dartmoor who suggested that the best way to cure whooping cough was to catch a house-mouse, fry it well and eat it. This remedy was amended somewhat by a Cotswold wise one who suggested that the mouse should be skinned and boned so that the patient didn't know what they were eating and that prospects for a complete recovery depended entirely upon the patient accepting the word of the wise woman that their 'meal' was an effective rural remedy.

Rheumatism is far from forgotten today and it is within living memory that a 'wise one' from near Washbourne is known to have recommended that "stinging nettles should be vigorously applied to the afflicted regions; this would certainly bring about relief". This is an ancient rural remedy that was well known in Roman times but less arduous was the more recent cure offered in Plymouth. Advisers in that city thought it only necessary for the patient to carry a nutmeg in their pocket to obtain relief. This may have had something to do with the local sales of imported nutmegs as once it was common practice simply to carry a potato to achieve a cure. People in the West Country who live near the moors are prone to claim that water from their local moor carries curative properties for rheumatics. Don't worry if you sneeze, for:

Sneeze on Monday, a sign of anger
Sneeze on Tuesday, kiss a stranger
Sneeze on Wednesday, hasty news
Sneeze on Thursday, love to choose
Sneeze on Friday, have a gift

Sneeze on Saturday, give a gift
Sneeze on Sunday, fresh and fasting,
Enjoy your true love for ever lasting.

There are many remedies recorded throughout the West Country for the removal of warts.

Get the sap out of a burning green stick and rub it on the warts while it is still hot. After three days the warts will go. (Penzance.)

Fast for three days. Each morning apply spittle to the warts. Fast again at the next full moon, apply the spittle and the warts will go away. (Street.)

Blow the warts towards the new moon, when you first see the next one. (Okehampton.)

The juice obtained from the stalks of the greater celandine and applied to warts will remove them. (Clovelly.) This cure was also commonly used in south Devon but was not apparently known to Culpeper, since it isn't mentioned by him.

Rub each wart with the velvet inner of a broadbean pod, then bury the pods. (Dorchester.) A variation to this remedy, from Wiltshire, is very elaborate and calls for a specifically sized package to be made, into which with due ceremonial the bean pods are secured and sealed with string, of particular length. The ritual is to be completed in secrecy, unobserved by others, and when completed the wart sufferer is instructed to take the package into a village or town, casually drop it, and scurry away to some place where it is possible, unseen, to observe but not identify the person who is curious enough to pick it up. They, poor innocents, will become Wiltshire's next wart sufferers, via the remedy's wart transfer system.

Wild thyme boiled in urine, with pepper, is another Wiltshire removal remedy.

Through the Quantocks, an ointment made from teasel root boiled to a pulp in urine is preferred.

Cut notches in an elder twig, equal in number to the total of warts to be removed, then throw the stick into a bramble bush. (Tetbury.) A lady who lived in the Cotswolds was said to be so proficient at wart removal with this stick method that doctors and nurses referred patients to her.

A treatment used in the Totnes area for an ulcerated leg is recorded as having been the application of 'cow dung'. Strained from straw and as fresh as it can possibly be, the cow dung cure is highly recommended by many a sufferer.

The use of cow droppings for other, more general cuts and wounds was recommended in the Newton Ferrers, Noss Mayo and Modbury areas where fresh dung was once regularly collected for use as a poultice.

THE FAMILY IN WASHBOURNE WOODS

Tales of the medical values of the ash tree are legendary, its leaves being used for poultices, balms or infusions, and its twigs for striking away warts or other blemishes. The tree itself is said to absorb sickness and illness if given the opportunity to help, and will give its own life if it fails.

Near Washbourne and Allaleigh there lived, not long ago, a family that relied upon the land for their livelihood. Few were the travellers who passed their door and while the markets at Totnes and Dartmouth were near enough to offer them the opportunity to trade their goods, they had little to spare beyond their needs. A whole year might come and go with nothing more that one visit to each town, if that. The family's piece of ground provided food enough for them and, by the standards of their own time when many scrounged, or suffered and starved in the cities, they lived quite well. The children's bellies were never empty, even if they were never fully filled. It was only when illness struck one of them down that the loneliness of the countryside became a cause for concern. Then the rural remedies of old came into use. Cures taught since childhood were recalled by the good wife and her husband. The wise woman who came by each year to help deliver, or bury, another babe was ever one to remind the wife of the country ways by which a life could be saved.

One day, as her youngest son lay fever ridden, coughing in his cot, the good wife remembered the remedies of old. She picked the child up gently and with her two young daughters close behind she hurried from their cottage and hastened towards the nearby woods. Her husband, axe in hand, watched their approach and silently pointed the way. Not a word was exchanged as the womenfolk hurried on, the stride of the girls not faltering as he handed them the axe. He turned, without a backward glance, to leave them to the spirits of the trees.

The woman tried to comfort the coughing child as they followed the axe marks her husband had made on the broad-leaved trees to lead them to where the young trees grew. At last, through sun-striped shadows they found what they required - young ash trees, growing straight and tall, but dividing where the axe could fall most easily, when wielded by a woman.

The girls selected one that suited their height and it split easily down the middle when the axe was swung first by one and then the other. The girls stood one each side of the tree and their mother handed the boy to one of them. The girl took her brother in her arms and handed him to her sister, through the tree. Three times the child was passed this way through the ash before he was handed back to his mother. The girls then gathered grasses and made a twist with which to bind the tree that it might heal itself more easily for they knew that, if the tree survived, so also would their brother as his sickness seeped into the tree, to stay where it could do no harm.

As they hurried home their worry was that if the sickness was too great, neither tree nor child would survive. They need not have feared the future though, for within the week the child's fever had passed and when they returned to see the tree they found it also thriving. Yet there was one thing to remind them of the ash tree cure. The young tree no longer stood so straight. Healed though it was it leaned one way a little, as if bearing a weight to one side. For those who journey through or explore the woods of Devon and see a listing ash tree , the question might be raised, is this an ash which, through taking sickness into itself and in return providing cures, was forced to grow this way?

9 The West Country's Favoured Fruit

The ancients believed that the fruit of the apple tree was given to their Gods to inhibit old age and, when the fruit was stolen, the Gods suffered that human frailty, until a successful seeker retrieved and returned the precious food. Symbolising fruitfulness, the apple was a feature of many beliefs. John Milton, author of *Paradise Lost*, reminded us that:

It was from out the rind of one apple tasted that the knowledge of
good and evil as two twins cleaving together leaped forth into the world.

Custom decrees, however, that there are everyday benefits to be gained from apple eating. As most people are aware, an apple a day keeps the doctor away but, in the West Country, it was more clearly shown that one person's good health was another's empty cupboard.

To eat an apple going to bed,
makes a doctor beg his bread.

Across the West County many came to rely upon the apple for a living and were never satisfied with just keeping practitioners of the medical profession at bay. When apple trees grew in profusion across the wooded landscape their produce, crushed and turned to liquid gold cider, was used to "warm the face, ease the throat, and keep the innards clear". In Marazion people used to cut an apple in two, rub one piece on warts, give that part to a pig to eat while they ate the other half of the apple. This should get rid of warts - but don't get the two pieces mixed up.

Should you be tempted to experiment, but you have any doubt about following that procedure, or you don't have a pig available, Newent offers an alternative. Cut an apple in two and rub each half over the warts. Tie the two halves together again with a piece of string and bury the apple. As the apple decays, so will the warts.

The importance of the apple was such that signs foretelling a good crop were eagerly awaited each year. If the trees bore blossom before April the prospect of fine fruit was not bright; better were their prospects if the blossom was delayed:

If apple blossom comes in March
For cider barrels don't you search.
When April brings the trees to bloom
The piper pays a merry tune.
But if all the trees bloom white in May
There'll be apples for cyder, and dumplings each day.

A crop in abundance could be relied upon in Somerset and Devon if, around 21 May, the Culmstock Fair came and went while there was blossom on the trees.

Till Culmstock Fair be come and gone
There may be apples or mid [might] be none.

The cider apple was not the only valued fruit. Crab apples too had their uses. Gathering the fruit from the hedgerows, maidens arranged it into the shape of their suitors' initials before safely hiding it away until 'old' Michaelmas Day. At dawn on 11 October, they would peep at the fruit to learn from the initials that had remained in the best condition which one of their suitors was to become their future husband.

> *Christmas time and little before,*
> *Eat the apple and throw the core;*
> *Christmas time and a little after,*
> *Eat the core, and the apple after.*

Whether this rhyme was another that helped people deal with doctors is not made clear but of one thing orchard keepers could be certain - if the sun was shining at 12 o'clock on Christmas Day, there would be a good crop of apples next year.

While today we can enjoy any number and variety of drinks, in those days when even water could be difficult to come by, the ales and ciders made around the country were vitally important to all people:

> *I like cider, an' cider likes me,*
> *I'll drink cider zo long as I can zee;*
> *I likes cider, an' cider likes I,*
> *An' I'll drink cider until I die.*

THE LURE OF LIQUID GOLD

Protecting the secrets that lie behind the making of cider became almost an occupation for some members of West Country families and some feared that if the Devil learned their secret ways in cider making he would offer that knowledge to the brewers of ale in return for their souls.

Cider makers in Devon consulted the white witch of the moors, who lived in the hills above Holne. His advice was freely given and was certainly followed. He told the makers of the golden drink that sulphur should be burnt while their cider making was in progress. This, the witch assured them, would keep the Devil at bay, ensuring that he would be unable to see what was being done, learn their secrets, or spoil their brew.

There is another long-held belief that it was the Devil himself who taught the monks of Tavistock to make cider sweet by burning brimstone. When asked about this belief a local landlord shook his head and replied, "I don't know about that, the cider around here is a devilishly good brew, but I've tasted better at the Church House at Holne." Whatever the Devil knew, the white witch of Holne seems to have kept some cider-making secrets to himself.

A visitor to Exmouth once recalled that he met a farmworker in the lanes on Woodbury Common and asked him the way to Otterton. The man, walking in that direction himself, offered to accompany the visitor and they chatted as they strolled together through the lanes in the summer sunshine. Passing a small roadside inn, the visitor invited his amiable companion to enter and slake his thirst. The offer was accepted and two pints of cider were called for.

Before putting the cooling brew to his lips, the labourer took up the mug and quite deliberately splashed some of the cider on to the floor of the inn as a libation for the Gods.

Walter Raymond, in his *Book of Simple Delights*, describes a carter halting his team at an inn door: "He took the cup and held it from him almost at arm's length. Then, with a slight quiver of the wrist, he spilt it, may have been a teaspoonful upon the ground. 'Here's luck,' cried he."

A Somerset man's advice to would-be cider drinkers:

Cider tap [top] *o' beer, be vurry gude cheer,*
Beer tap o' cider be a vurry bad rider.

Many Somerset farmworkers believed that tea was not good for the liver. If a good wife brought them tea in the fields, a drink of cider was the cure recommended and taken before work resumed.

Further advice to cider drinkers:

When the cider's in the can, the wit is in the man;
When the cider's in the man, the wit is in the can.

At Bow, well within living memory, at haymaking time before their first meal in the field the farmhands threw a few crumbs on the ground and sprinkled a few drops of cider around the field for 'the little people'to ensure their blessing of a good harvest.

When taking a drop o'cider, don't ever forget the fairies!

THE ALE MAKER OF TAW VALLEY

St Dunstan's Day, 19 May, was marked and enjoyed by many ale makers in the kingdom but some in Devon believed that the saint had agreed to sell his soul to the Devil in return for the Devil giving his help to Dunstan's ale-making friends. For them, St Franklin's night, celebrated on 19 May, became a reminder of that contract with the Devil, made by a brewer who was by no means a saint.

A brewer of ale, by the name of Frankan, or Franklin, once lived and worked in the Taw Valley near the village of Eggesford in an area where cider was the popular local drink, and cider making was a successful and rewarding business.

The brewmaster was a coarse and surly man who did little to encourage friendships but kept himself to himself year after lonely year. As his ales fermented, so did his jealousy. Demand for his ales continued, but each year the demand dropped a little more. He began to envy the wealth being gained by others but, when he grudgingly gave time to talking with his neighbours, he invariably ended up arguing with them. He adamantly refused even to consider their suggestions that he should give up brewing ale, and join them in their cider making.

As his business withered away his clothes became more ragged while, to his eyes, the cider makers appeared to flaunt their wealth before him as they passed along the valley cloaked in ever finer cloth and riding in finely appointed carriages drawn by magnificent white stallions. Their extravagances were like barbs to the brewer of ale, striking deep into his heart. He cursed and swore at anyone who dared to approach him and responded with lewd gestures to those who, occasionally, raised a jewelled hand to acknowledge his presence with the briefest sign as their curtained carriage passed by. Eventually, hardly anyone bothered to acknowledge him any longer and fewer still called upon him. Children were warned not to go near him or his home. Weeks passed quite often without him speaking to another living soul until he delivered a barrel of ale somewhere; and such deliveries were seldom enough.

A mule had long since replaced the last horse he had owned and he spent much of his time riding, some might say hiding, in the hills.

One day, from high on the ridge above the valley, he looked down to where the apple blossom hung on the trees, glowing in the light of a fine May morning, mocking him, drawing from his curled lips a curse on its beauty, and on the profit it promised to others. The tormented brewmaster vowed then that the Devil could take his soul if he would enter into a compact with him. He implored the beast of hell to destroy the apple blossom there and then, and to destroy it every year that he lived, until it was time for him to pay off his debts. Swirling mists drifted in from two moors as the brewer returned to his home: the Devil had heard his plea.

That night, and for two nights following, frost settled in the Taw Valley devastating the apple blossom and destroying any prospect for cider making later in the year. Like many who live by the land the cider makers respected nature, tightened their belts and waited for a better crop the next year. To their dismay the frosts came again late in May the following year, and the year after that and every year until cider making in the valley became almost a memory for everyone. There was one exception, a wealthy brewer of ale who was reminded by the frosts each year that he owed his prosperity to the Devil, reminded by the frosts of 'Francimass' or 'St Franklin's Nights', as three frosty nights late in May became known. Only when that brewer died did the regularity of the frosts cease, but by then the apple orchards had been uprooted since, always afflicted by the frost, they never bore a crop.

Tall trees now grow in the valley where apple orchards once stood but when the frosts occasionally appear on three consecutive nights in May, near the 19th, 20th or 21st, intruders beware. It is said that a man on a mule might be encountered among the trees on the ridge when the brewmaster, a tortured soul, returns from another world to seek someone who will take on his burden. In those three days he must find another soul to send back in his place, or else he must return once again to continue his eternal contract with the Devil.

DRINK TO THE FREEDOM OF SLAVES

It was known far and wide that the West Country apple orchards produced the best cider in the world and that the secrets of the cider makers had been passed down from parent to child for centuries. Ale makers could not brew an ale which compared in quality to the sweet apple ciders of the South-West region and they tried in many ways to obtain the recipe for success enjoyed by the cider makers.

One ale maker, much against his son's wishes, sent the young man to sea for a couple of years to serve aboard a merchant ship which was known to trade with Spain and Africa. After being burned by the sun, the winds and the salt sea for years the father believed that, on his return, his son would be seen as a sailor, and not recognised as a local lad. He instructed his son that when his term at sea was served he was to make his way from Plymouth around the West Country telling a tale or two as sailors do, staying a while here, offering a helping hand there, particularly where the cider apples grew, to gain the confidence of those who knew the secrets of cider making. With money in his pocket and a strong arm, the daughters of the cider makers would certainly have their eyes on him. Their fathers would recognise a work-horse in waiting, and would encourage him to give up the sea and settle down. By such devious means the ale maker hoped that his son would learn the secret of sweet cider making and make him a rich man by doing so. What the cunning rogue had failed to consider was that his son would take to a liking the sea, like many a West Countryman before him.

The lad left Plymouth in the early spring, on a merchant ship with sails set for Cadiz, or so he thought. There was to be no Spanish destination. Unwittingly, the ale maker had secured his son's services to a slave-trader. In the fourth month of the thirtieth year of the nineteenth century the youth left this island under billowing sails that were to take him first to Africa where he was forced to watch as a human cargo was pushed and shoved into the hold of the ship. The thrill of the voyage, the heat of the day, the majesty of Africa, all were lost to the youth as he watched the misery etched into the faces of those who were pushed roughly aboard.

Men, women, children, babes in arms, with bowed heads and downcast eyes, some with arms bound behind them, others roped by the neck or chained together, all shuffled forward without a glance to left or right as they were herded beneath the decks to be secured, for safety's sake. Sickened by the sight, but fearful for his own life, the boy volunteered help to the ship's cook, and stole food for others. He watched again as the survivors were ushered ashore to a new land, before he too fled the ship, intent on righting a wrong.

It was the early organisers of an anti-slavery society who found a willing work-horse. Having set himself up as an ale maker in America the boy was by 1836 urging people to follow the route towards abolition. His business prospered and by 1843 his own merchant ship was plying the coast of his new country for trade. It was to be twenty years more however before Abraham Lincoln issued the Emancipation Proclamation, two years into a bitter civil war; and the Constitution of the country he had adopted as his own was amended to abolish slavery just three days before he died.

10 Baby Talk

Many of the old beliefs about babies, births and baptisms still survive in the West Country and are actively followed. In the Cotswolds it was a common belief that a baby's first journey must be upwards, and to lift the newborn babe was the first action of the person delivering the child, an action not unknown in the modern maternity unit.

It was widely believed that holy water sprinkled around a cradle would avert the evil eye and prevent a child from being 'overlooked'. Holy water was so sought after at times that fonts were often kept locked to prevent the water being stolen.

The arrival of a baby has always been a time for gifts and, should you be invited to visit friends who have recently become parents, go prepared with something of silver to give the newborn child and ensure the old custom continues. In the eighteenth century silver threepenny bits were the favourite gift. Nowadays, since we no longer have silver coins, the custom is more often continued with the gift of a silver bowl, cup, ring or trinket. If the child immediately clutches the coin or gift when it is offered, it is a sign that it will thrive and grow rich.

In Cornwall, tradition walked side by side with the baby's mother when she first went to be 'churched' or 'upraised' - blessed in church after giving birth. A 'groaning cake', was made after the baby was born for every visitor to share. The mother carried some with her on her first visit to church, to share with anyone she met on her way there and the cake, sometimes known as 'kimbly cake', was also carried by the parents when they took the baby to church for its christening. In January 1884, a magistrate wrote to the *Western Morning News* to say that while on his way to his petty sessions he had crossed the path of a baptismal party and the parents had stopped him to thrust this special christening cake into his hand to make sure that he did not pass the child without having some.

It is now thought to be lucky if a baby being baptised cries as soon as the sign of the cross is made upon it. The origins lie in the belief that only if this happened would those around them be sure that the Devil had been thwarted, and had departed from the innocent child.

Some residents around Salcombe say that at services where more than one child is baptised, the baby baptised first will never serve, or be subservient to, those baptised after it.

The christening gown, and/or shawl, is something still in use, but in Dorset the christening 'palm' was used. One, already quite old, was described in 1875 in *Notes and Queries* as being "some 5 feet in length, and a little less in breadth, made of a rich crimson satin, lined with pink lace now somewhat faded, with a double edging of what seems to be silver lace". A correspondent suggested that the palm was not used only for the baptism of infants but was also more regularly used to wrap up the child when it was taken out. In Devon, the christening 'pane', or 'pame', appears to have been the equivalent.

For some unmarried young people in Somerset and Cornwall who were called upon to become Godparents to the newborn baby the prospect was not always appealing. "First at the font, never at the altar", was a very real concern of young men as well as young women.

For two unmarried people to be seen together at the font, two alternative comments can be considered. In Cornwall we were told that this was unlucky for them both and that neither one nor the other would ever marry. In Somerset it was taken as a certain sign that to the font they would return, married, and with a child of their own.

There is a custom known countrywide, and often followed, that mothers, or fathers, bite off instead of cut their baby's nails. This was defined further in some areas of Devon where it was said that the biting custom must be followed, and scissors must not be used for the first six months if the child was to be saved from becoming 'light-fingered' later on.

At Stoke Fleming, even greater precaution was taken to avoid such potential problems because in that area it was considered essential that the nail chewing should continue for a whole year.

Birthmarks, it was once believed, could be removed by the 'fasting' spittle of the mother. This remedy would also cure a baby that was suffering from an eye-cold and problems such as squint eyes were expected to be resolved by the application of spit.

Adults and children suck or lick their own wounds automatically. A cut, a splinter, a bruise, a battered thumb, all respond to spittle - the memory of ancient ways continues. From the moment of birth, we live in a world surrounded by folklore and once in a while those age old remedies suddenly take on a modern mantle, as recorded in the *Daily Mail* of 13 June 1997:

Licked Clean

Licking your wounds may help to heal them, according to a study in the medical journal, 'The Lancet', today. The instinctive action helps kickstart an anti-infection process. Saliva contains nitrite, which reacts with the acid on the skin's surface to form nitric oxide, a powerful microbe killer.

NITTY GRITTY FOLKLORE

Head lice have caused havoc in households for centuries but it is not that long ago that mothers following medical folklore were feeding their children sulphur tablets at the end of March as a treatment for the infestation. They also used flowers of sulphur baths, to stop the itching which was likely to be caused by scabies.

Persistent 'head visitors' were winkled out with a scalp-piercing nit-comb.

A worried mother, egged on by her other children standing a safe distance from the victim, would wield the weapon with maniacal dexterity during a frenzied chase after the pin-head rogues, and then try to stop the wounds that she had inflicted from festering by dousing them with vinegar and water.

The word soon spread when 'Nitty Nora' was expected to be coming to school. Her imminent arrival inspired some, worried others and challenged a few. To teachers and school staff the woman appeared as a saintly nurse, arriving to relieve them of their troubles. To the impressionable and younger population of the school she came as a witch, or worse. To the older children, Nitty Nora's fearful beckoning finger did not pull them to their doom but to an opportunity of a day or two off school while 'the treatment' was undertaken, with hair washed in paraffin or other peculiar products. Many in this latter group prepared themselves for the examination by rubbing heads with the infested, thus hopefully ensuring they received sufficient hair-born visitations to guarantee them their days away from the tedium of school.

11 Feathered Folk

The sound of birds is a pleasure to any who enjoy the countryside, and in the West Country, like all regions, the homebirds and regularly returning visitors have added more than a note or two to folklore, custom and local traditions.

BLUETITS
The Devonshire name for bluetits, 'accymal', is said to derive from *ecce mal* (behold the bad), the bird being condemned for having attacked the eyes of Christ as he suffered on the cross. 'Hickmall', 'hackmal', heckymal', 'hagmal', 'hackeymal' and 'titmal' are some of the variations on the name used across Devon and in the West Country.

The Reverend Charles Swainson suggested in *The Folk Lore and Provincial Names of British Birds* (1886) that the story arose from the strong pecks that the bird can deal out with its bill.

CRANES AND HERONS
Across the West Country we have met many great 'local' predictors of weather conditions, some of whom associated future conditions with the flight of cranes or herons. In Devon, when cranes at Huntingdon Warren needed to go downstream to fish it was taken as a sign that bad weather was approaching, but see them flying upstream to fish and fine weather is following them.

CROWS
A single crow seen in Somerset is an ill omen, but it takes three crows seen together in the Hartland area of Devon to be regarded as heralds of misfortune.

There is a belief around North Bovey that when an old crow sits on a bough and croaks continually, someone nearby is going to die. This is a belief shared across the South West. People living along the Severn, near Ashleworth, having their attention attracted to the croaking crow also take particular notice of the direction it takes when it flies away because, we were told, that will show which way the funeral procession will come from.

Crows appear to be regarded with fear all over the world if Butler, writing in 'Hudinbras' is to be believed:

Is it not om'nous in all countries
When crows and ravens croak upon trees?

CUCKOOS
The cuckoo has its own calendar for arrival and departure, with regional variations. In Devon it is made quite clear that:

In March he begin'th to larch,
In April he open'th his bill,
In May he sing'th all day,
In June he alter'th his tune,
In July away he doth fly.

This indicates some favouritism on the bird's part since either side of Devon, in both Dorset and Cornwall, the cuckoo, according to their version of the rhyme, doesn't arrive until April. It does stay until August to balance things up though and, in whichever four months it is present, there is much to remember about the bird.

According to residents of East Devon it is necessary, the first time you hear a cuckoo, to run and kiss a gate post; this will attract earnings and you will not be idle all year. Others, in West Devon, say that to kiss the post and sit on the gate is what is required to ensure a year of good earnings, but we suspect the added suggestion was made by those who were tired after running some distance to a gate when hearing the cuckoo in the first place.

While keen Devon gardeners are advised to rush off and plant runner beans in March, as soon as any gardener in Gloucestershire and Somerset hears the call of the cuckoo a month later, its welcome cry brings beans to their mind and they too respond to the reminder to get them planted without delay, to ensure a full-flavoured crop.

If gardening is not your interest, you could at least turn your money over in your pocket when you first hear the cuckoo, to encourage the money to increase and to bring you good fortune.

If you haven't any money it is probably advisable to run off to the nearest gate post, especially if you are near Callington when you hear it for the first time and the cuckoo is calling in front of you. Around there, it is a sign that you will be fortunate, and will rise up in the world.

The cuckoo in Devon is blamed for stealing the colour blue from clothes when that colour faded and, early in the year when weather was not at its best, parents in Kingsbridge were admonished not to let their children go into muddy lanes until "the cuckoo comes and licks up the mud". Many a harassed mother must have been relieved to hear the call of the cuckoo heralding the arrival of warmer, drier days.

There is a warning in Dorset that if you don't turn round and run when you first hear the cuckoo you will end up in debt before the year is out. If you do run, whatever your wish it shall be granted.

In Torquay the cuckoo is held to be one of the 'seven sleepers', the tortoise and snake being two of the others, and almost any hibernating animal is said to make up the remainder of the 'seven sleepers'.

On the Teign, fisherpeople claim that cuckoos call the salmon up over the weir. And on the banks of the Severn it is said that the fish swim further upriver after they hear the cuckoo call.

In the Tiverton area a local tale dating from antiquity tells of a cuckoo released from a box each year around mid-April from the tower of Poughill church so that it could attend Witheridge fair, held some six miles distant.

When the cuckoo returns each year to the countryside the unmistakable song is taken as a signal for so much to start again each spring; and from its song springs hope eternal.

In 'Shepherd's Week', John Gay's fourth *Pastoral*, the writer refers to a

custom well known in his native Devon in which a maiden looks in her shoe
for a clue to the identity of her future husband:

> When first the year I heard the cuckoo sing,
> And call with welcome note the budding spring,
> I straightway set a-running with such haste,
> Deb'rah that ran the smock scarce ran so fast;
> Till, spent for lack of breath, quite weary grown,
> Upon a rising bank I sat down,
> And doff'd my shoe, and by my troth I swear,
> Therein I spied this yellow frizzled hair,
> As like to Lubberkin's in curl and hue,
> As if upon his comely pate it grew.

In some areas of Devon the cuckoo was believed to be the same bird as the
sparrowhawk and both Pliny and Aristotle mention in their writings the
ancient belief that the cuckoo, during a portion of the year, was converted
into a bird of prey.

The cuckoo, despite its reputation as a tyrant that forces its young on
others, is that 'different' bird whose arrival is always noticed, noticed and
remembered even to the time of day by many. People with no interest in
folklore, who scarcely care that a swallow and a seagull differ, will make a
point of mentioning precisely when they hear the first cuckoo. Even among
the country folk though, few will know that it is only the male cuckoo who
calls out its own name, but with each return of his welcome cry the old customs
carry on again.

CURLEWS

The weather forecasters around Huntingdon Warren considered that, when
they saw curlews flying away from the moor towards the country, it was a
sign of bad weather. When they observed the curlews flying from the country
towards the moor, good weather could be expected.

JACKDAWS

Along parts of the North Cornwall and North Devon coastline from Tintagel to Baggy Point we heard that the jackdaw, although being quite a distinct bird, was sometimes considered to be a young rook, giving rise to the Hartland saying, "A jackdaw is the worst rook out".

If regional residents heard a jackdaw calling down their chimney, they could expect trouble to follow. One jackdaw seen perched on each pinnacle on the tower of Hartland church on a Sunday was taken as a clear indication that there would be a funeral service in the church before the next Sunday came around.

At Newquay a jackdaw settling on the headstone of a grave was said to be warning of a funeral.

LAPWINGS

When the lapwing is observed taking its leave from any of the open West Country moorland and seeking shelter in countryside that provides convenient cover, or if any are observed biding their time beneath the eaves and beside the walls of village cottages, be sure to go out well prepared with waterproof clothing, for the foulest of weather can be expected.

MAGPIES

Many people when seeing some magpies remember the old rhyme, usually accounting for as many as four. Few get as far as some people in Cornwall:

> *One for sorrow*
> *Two for mirth*
> *Three for a wedding*
> *Four for a birth*
> *Five for Heaven*
> *Six for Hell*
> *The seventh takes your soul to the Devil to sell.*

There are regional variations but, in Devon for a person to avoid the ill fortune attributed to the single bird encountered on the ground, it is considered wise that they should spit over their right shoulder three times, and each time repeat the words:

> *Unclean by twos,*
> *worse still by sevens,*
> *The one I choose*
> *Is the one in the heavens.*

The Cornish always remember to doff their hats if worn to magpies or bow the head if not, as this form of recognition turns away harm.

The woman with a bitter tongue is spoken of as being a 'magpie' in Cornwall, and as a 'madg', meggie', or 'maggie' in some other parts of the West Country.

A Dorset worker would very soon become concerned if the magpie stays nearby while they work throughout the day: they would believe that their days on earth are almost an end.

Throughout the region it was agreed that to kill a magpie was one of the unluckiest things anybody could do and there is a general 'fear' of the birds even though they supposedly bring benefits with them four times out of seven.

PEACOCKS
Coryton farmers say that it is very unlucky to take peacock feathers indoors, but in some areas of the county they are often used for ornament or decoration. The birds themselves have earned a good reputation for guarding property and, while one owner was convinced that they kept the Devil at bay by distracting his attention with their fine plumage, we suspect that this idea returned with him after his years overseas in the Far East, where the birds originated.

PIGEONS
The wild variety of pigeon is often considered a pest when taking up residence in a public place but when pigeons are seen to roost on the roof of a residence occupied by a newly wed couple the local tongues will soon wag. The presence of such a pigeon pair is known to be a sign that the marriage will be blessed with happiness, and many, many children.

With the forecast fulfilled, the couple might have a need for peaceful nights themselves and be glad to lay their weary heads on soft pillows. Pigeon feather pillows however cannot be recommended if custom is correct since pillows filled with pigeon feathers are said to be a cause of insomnia, and worse - they could bring death to those who use them.

You should try not to view a pigeon through glass. If seen flying across, or very close, to a window, it is said that the pigeon is prophesying problems.

RAVENS
Of all birds, the raven, or at least its cry, was most disliked. Anyone who has heard the coarse call of the big black bird will know that its cry sounds like 'corpse, corpse', and will understand more readily why, in all West Country counties and far beyond, the bird is considered to be an omen of death, or one that brings bad luck.

A raven resting on top of a church tower is said to be watching for the death that will occur within the week.

A raven croaking as it flies over a house is foretelling the death of a resident there and forecasting that the death will occur within twenty-four hours.

A raven flying around a house is a sign that a corpse will soon depart the premises.

Even faced with this, West Country people must still have a lot less to worry about than anyone who lives near the Tower of London, where the raven is encouraged to remain, to keep England safe.

ROBINS
Robins are among the most inquisitive and friendly of British birds, ever ready to make a human friend and, though always cautious, the robin seems to stay

once friendship is made.

It has, however, a reputation for over-eating, earned it is said from its ability to consume twice its own weight in one day, and referred to clearly in a Cornish couplet:

Robins first eat the pews and then the steeple
And, if not shot, the parson and people.

A robin entering a house is considered to bring misfortune with it. In Devon a robin heard crying at the door was a sign of sorrow, while in Gloucestershire one tapping at the window was warning of a death nearby. In both regions, a robin seen to fly indoors was regarded as one signalling that death would arrive there swiftly and unexpectedly; 'hopping' over the threshold it was bringing in debt. During November however, by whichever means the robin entered the house that month, it was considered to be bringing good luck to the home, and not heralding a death or misfortune.

West Country farmers encouraged robins to feed with their poultry, as payment in advance for services rendered. They were anticipating that the robin would warn them if foxes were about.

The robin and the wren are often associated together in nursery lore, where they are known as Cock Robin and Jenny Wren:

The robin and the wren
Are God Almighty's cock and hen.

So sacred were they regarded that a Cornish warning was added:

Strub a robin or wran
Then never prosper, boy nor man.

ROOKS

Rooks always did, and still do, provide many a countrydweller with their weather forecast, well in advance.

When they build nests deep into a tree, close in to the trunk, a bad summer can be expected. Nests built far out on the extremities of branches indicate good weather for the coming summer. Picnickers might note that in Somerset it is said that the birds will desert an unsafe tree.

As daily forecasters of weather conditions the sight of rooks wheeling and cawing in a state of agitation is a sure sign of rain to knowledgeable country dwellers. The appearance of a black and white rook foretells disaster.

In the Cotswolds the belief continues that rooks nesting near people will forsake their rookery if ill fortune is to strike those they live near, and the relationship appears to extend to a sharing of sorrow at times of bereavement for when a death occurs it has often been known that rooks will leave the area and not return until after the funeral.

SWALLOWS

The arrival of the high-flying swallow is always viewed with pleasure, since the bird is believed to be welcoming the better weather that is also due to arrive, but when the bird swoops low it is not such a welcome sight because it is clearly trying to avoid the impending storms.

In the past, workmen in Little Torrington considered that they could be reasonably sure of getting paid for work they were doing on a house if swallows were seen building their nests under its eaves. This was a sign that the person living there was making money.

For energetic beekeepers in Devon the swallow holds out hope. If you run when you see your first swallow and you jump over a 'vreth' (a wreathed or wattled hurdle) or a five-barred gate, you will find a swarm of bees before the year ends.

Swallows return to the same place year after year. A single swallow is a sign of a wedding soon to be bless'd. Courting couples living near Newent watched for the first lone arrival to see if it found a mate and thus forecast their own future happiness. In Dorset, married couples awaited the return of a pair of swallows. If the birds successfully reared a family the couple's life would be similarly blessed before the birds returned next year.

12 Rogationtide and Beating the Bounds

Determined by the dates of Easter, which itself is determined by the moon, Rogationtide follows on five weeks later and consists of Rogation Sunday together with the following Monday, Tuesday and Wednesday, four days in all immediately preceding Ascension Day.

Rogation ritual and custom predate Christianity, but the ancient practice of seeking blessings from the Gods upon the newly sown crops or, around the West Country coasts, of calling upon the water deities to provide fish in abundance, soon became incorporated in the new religion.

The ancient tribal Dumnonii marked out their lands across the moors and countryside over two thousand years ago, the Saxons clearly staked their claims to land and defined boundaries, and after the Reformation, when many religious customs disappeared, even the clergy were permitted to 'beat the bounds' in the traditional manner and offer prayers along the way. In 1652 George Herbert wrote in *The Country Parson* of four advantages to be gained from their doing so:

> 1, a blessing of God for the fruits of the field; 2, Justice in the preservation of bounds; 3, Charitie, in living, walking and neighbourly accompanying one an other, with reconciling of differences at that time, if there be any; 4, Mercie, in relieving the poor by a liberal distribution of largess which at that time is or ought to be made.

Beating the bounds of an area of land, usually a parish, flourishes in the West Country and very often takes place on or around Rogationtide. Parishioners of South Tawton maintain the tradition every seven years and on Saturday 7 May 1994 an estimated three hundred people set out from South Zeal to 'beat the bounds' in time-honoured manner as the brief report that appeared in the *Okehampton Times* on 12 May indicates:

> With a spirit that has survived two thousand years and more, parishioners of South Tawton took to the moors on May 7th to mark their boundaries. They set out from South Zeal, accompanied by visitors from across the county and far be yond, with almost St Crispian day thoughts that those 'now abed, shall think themselves accurs'd they were not here', to march on Mill Farm, where Mr and Mrs Clarke continued tradition by letting one, representing all, walk through their home to mark the boundary line within. Onwards to Raybarrow stone, above Shilley Pool, where Hannah Tudor Wilson, the youngest child present, and Megan Pillar the youngest walker, aged four, were each seated on the stone and 'bounced' seven times upon it to ensure that they would know the place in future years. Septuagenarian villager, Mr Gerald Jeffries, was similarly ceremonially seated to remind all present that traditions pass from age to age. Possible intruders from Throwleigh were warned off, passing mire and marshlands miles of moorland were crossed to remind Belstone of South Tawton's 'rights', before walkers wended their way through Skaigh Cleave to Sticklepath. Their lands secured, parishioners returned to South Zeal, triumphant in having preserved a piece of England in just a few short hours.

Traditionally a moorland feast takes place near one of the boundary markers but on this occasion the boundary beaters returned to South Zeal to a prepared ram roast and other foods.

13 Some More Snippets of Folklore

Around Buckfast it still considered by many folk there to be unlucky if new shoes are placed upon the table. A follower of folklore in South Devon once told us that harm would certainly befall any person who, when taking their shoes off at night, failed after removing them to place them immediately upside down with the soles up in the air. Whenever the opportunity has arisen we've discreetly observed friends, relatives and sometimes visitors remove their shoes but we've yet to find anyone who observes the warning - but they've all managed to survive.

Not every omen offers only doom and gloom. In Sherford, Strete, Slapton, Stokenham and South Allington they burn a boot on Christmas Eve to keep shoe leather on their feet and health enough to wear it well throughout the next year.

In some areas it was thought that if a farmer's wife let her kettle boil dry it would cause the cows to go dry too but around Bigbury it was said that when a cow was milked not into a pail but on to the ground the cow would then surely go dry.

Sewing on a Sunday was something to be frowned upon. "Every stitch you take up on a Sunday pricks our Lord" is a South Devon saying. Many rural residents have a Sunday fear that warns them against ever using scissors on the Sabbath, while the cutting of hair or nails is never recommended for a Friday.

Signs and omens could be seen wherever one looked and not long ago it was known that when the hem of a lady's skirt turned up of its own accord it meant that she would soon receive a letter. If someone else first noticed that the lady's skirt had 'rucked' and went to her assistance, that helper would receive the letter instead.

Visiting a friend's home could invoke disaster because it was once commonly understood that for a guest to sit down upon a chair from which someone else had just risen was an omen of their imminent death and that they were ready to step into their own grave.

In ancient days when it was believed that everyday items could make or mar the future, reveal prospects for prosperity or marriage, and provide an ample portion of good luck if treated correctly, everything around was regarded in ways that differ today. It was once believed that a piece of metal should be worn constantly as a protection against the evil eye. Those days have long gone and won't return again. You can bet your lucky coin, rub your medallion, or touch your talisman, on that.

In North Devon it is believed that fruit stains on tablecloths or linen cannot be removed, no matter how hard you try, until the season for the fruit that caused the stain is over.

The following item, like much folklore, makes some sense if you look beyond the first thing you come across.

I saw the village-pond burning with fire.
I saw a thatched cottage bowing to a squire.
I saw a parson twelve feet high.

I saw a balloon made of lead.
I saw a coffin drop down dead.
I saw two pigeons run a race.
I saw two donkeys making lace.
I saw a maiden with a face like a cat.
I saw a kitten wear a straw hat.
I saw a man who saw these too.
Who said it's strange but they're all true.

(Still not clear? Start again and pull out all stops to ensure success.)

Between 1645 and 1895 three incumbents held the living of Bampton for an average of nearly sixty years each. 'Old Bart Davey', instituted in the middle of George III's reign, survived until the eighth year of Queen Victoria's rule. An irreverent parishioner rudely disturbed the sabbatic calm of Bampton by nailing this ditty to the church door:

The Parson is wored out
The Clerk is most ado;
The Saxton's gude vor nort -
'Tis time uz have all new.

An acrostic ballad written by the vicar of Winsford in 1906-ish:

Where the swift Exe, by Somerset's fair hills,
In curving eddies borders pastures deep
Near fern-tinged slopes of lawn, where babbling rills
Sing sweetest music, 'mid thick foliage peep
Five bridges, and thatched roofs. The grey Church Tower
O 'er all looks down on groves of oak and pine;
Red deer, red Devon's ponies of the moor,
Delight the traveller in this home of mine.

An Exeter poem, reported as being heard in July 1850:

Snail, snail, shut out your horns;
Father and mother are dead:
Brother and sister are in the back yard
Begging for barley bread.

The twentieth century is catching up on folklore, as reported in the *Daily Mail* of 25 June 1997:

Find New Love with Herb from the Past

A herbal medicine used in the Middle Ages could help revive women's love lives after the menopause according to new research. Extracts of the plant St John's Wort - Hypericum perforatum - were given to women who complained they no longer felt attractive and had lost interest in sex. After taking hypericum tablets for three months, more than two thirds of 111 women who saw their doctors with menopausal problems felt desirable again, while only 15 percent still put sex low on their priorities. The supplement, already a proven antidepressant with fewer side effects than man-made drugs, helped boost the women's self-esteem and confidence . . . Hypericum tablets are sold in Britain through health food shops and are not licensed as prescription drugs.

14 A Few Helpful Herbs and Plants

Even in the modern world it is simply not possible to pass through any day or walk through any way without being close to the lore of ancient times. The wise ones of the past, who were often feared as witches for practising their craft, used only the things close to hand to help themselves and those who trusted them. Today we rely upon the drugs industry and the supermarket and forget too easily that the wisdom of ancient times is still around us.

NETTLES
Nettles had many domestic values as well as being widely used for remedial purposes.

Nettle oil preceded paraffin, the juice of nettles was used to curdle milk and nettle cheese has regained a widespread West Country popularity in recent years.

Nettles could also be used to seal cracks in leaking tubs or barrels. Hung in the larder nettles deter flies and, near bee-hives, they repel frogs (frogs were considered a predator that made a meal of any bee that stood for too long at the entrance to a hive).

Either as a drink or as a poultice, nettles were commended to relieve pleurisy. The recipe for a drink was:

Place freshly picked nettle leaves in a saucepan, add a pint of water and boil for 15 minutes. Dose: half to one teaspoonful, three times daily.

Take boiling hot nettle leaves to make a poultice; when cold, put the poultice on a cloth, place it over the pain, and cover with oilcloth.

A decoction popular in the Cotswolds was shredded nettles mixed in wine. The drink was 'guaranteed' to provoke urine, expel stones, kill worms in children and dissolve windiness in the spleen.

The white nettle is sometimes called white archangel and is said to bloom around 8 May, the Feast of St Michael on the 'old' calendar.

MANDRAKE ROOT
The shape of the mandrake root made this a favoured plant for rituals intended to improve the fertility of a male.

It is recognised and appreciated in Somerset and Dorset for encouraging passion and helping love-making.

Roots which grew in the shadow of the gallows were considered to hold the soul of those who died by the rope. They would never find rest until the root was removed. Dealt with only after sunset, the screaming root was drawn from the ground not by human hand but by the power of a hungry dog. Tied to the plant, the animal was enticed forward by offering it a meat-bone until it pulled the root from the earth and released the entrapped soul of the departed.

MUGWORT

While the mugwort plant is considered across the Cotswolds to offer protection against witches, the hiker may have regard for another belief found in the area. Mugwort placed in walking boots will make each and every mile seem half its length. Walking on a cushion of mugwort is recommended as a means of offsetting fatigue.

DEADLY AND WOODY NIGHTSHADE

Through all the country the nightshade twins, deadly and woody, have an evil reputation. Used by witches, deadly induces madness or death, and provides them with the power to fly. Used by farmers, however, a collar of nightshade was said to save cattle from enchantment and, twisted in a wreath with holly, to be a cure for hag-ridden horses. Humans could wear a wreath of the woody plant around their brow to defeat spells.

The distilled juice of this herb was used to relieve the swelling of testicles, did good for ringworm and shingles and, dropped into the ears, eased pains that arose from inflammation. It was also good for swelling under the throat. However, since both nightshades are poisonous, *do not touch them*.

Culpeper, the most renowned collector of herbal lore, warns of the perils that just the touch of deadly nightshade can inflict.

A lady, troubled by a small ulcer below one of her eyes, applied a portion of green deadly nightshade leaf to it one night and, by morning, the uvea, the posterior covering of the iris, was so affected that the pupil would not contract in the brightest light. Fortunately, her other eye remained unaffected and when the piece of leaf was removed from the ulcer the afflicted eye was gradually restored to its original state.

PENNYROYAL

Pennyroyal is known in some areas of Devon as 'organs', and the herb is still widely used in the West Country for making a 'tea' that is considered to be both stimulating to the spirit and helpful in overcoming lethargy.

In Ashburton, pennyroyal was used to make 'organ broth' and, when tea cost sixpence an ounce and coffee threepence, organ broth, or pennyroyal tea, with ingredients easily available locally, was more popular than either.

Wise women in country areas kept a good stock of pennyroyal to give to the ladies who needed their services during pregnancy. It helped them gain strength and eased the pains of childbirth.

SOUTHERNWOOD

Southernwood has, among many others, three customary values that appear particularly promising.

For women, the main value of this plant is that they can carry it as their predecessors did to sniff and offset drowsiness.

For men, ashes of southernwood mixed with old salad oil is recommended for baldness because custom has it that it can cause hair to grow again on the head or chin.

It is also recommended, to any male or female who is incarcerated for a considerable period due to a life of crime, that southernwood should be kept in their dungeon or prison cell, as a remedy for jail-fever.

ST JOHN'S WORT

St John's Wort is a herb associated everywhere with midsummer and its rituals, and can be relied upon to banish ghosts, witches, devils and imps, when set in the window on 24 June, the martyred saint's 'day'. Added to this, its presence in a house provides reliable protection against fires or lightning.

A childless wife who, respectfully and with due ceremony on St John's Eve, 23 June, walks naked to pick the wort when the dew is still on it, can be assured, like her sisters in centuries past, that she will conceive within a year.

VALERIAN

A girl who wears of sprig of valerian will never lack lovers for this is the strongest plant for provoking love and was used as a love potion and aphrodisiac throughout the West Country.

Topsell's *Four Footed Beasts*, published in 1658, confirms that cats are fond of valerian. He advises that:

> The root of the herb Valerian (called Phu) is very like to the eye of a cat, and wheresoever it groweth, if cats come thereunto, they instantly dig it up for the love thereof, as I myself have seen in mine own garden, for it smelleth moreover like a cat.

As the rhyme has it:

> If you set it, the cats will eat it;
> If you sow it, the cats will know it.

15 A Folklore Bouquet

Take a walk along a West Country lane and look into the gardens, the hedgerow, the field, copse or wood, and in every place a veritable bouquet of folklore beckons.

BIRD'S EYE
The small, blue, pretty hedgerow flower, bird's eye, was one that was avoided by children in the area of Bow, in Devon, as they walked to school. Only the bravest, or the most foolhardy, among them would even approach the plant, let alone actually pick it, because their parents had warned them of the horrible fate that would befall them if they plucked it from the ground. "A robin will come down and peck out your eyes" was one of the most frightening prospects and "you'll get the king's evil" was another. Around Brewham and Wincanton too, the warnings of what birds would do to young eyes helped ensure that the plant remained untouched in those areas by inquisitive youngsters.

BLUEBELLS
For no apparent reason, or one not apparent nowadays, the bluebell is one of those flowers considered by custom to be unlucky if brought indoors. During the Middle Ages it was a flower much sought after by bowmen, who extracted sap from the plant to make a gum which they used to fix feathers for flights on to the shafts of their arrows. This connection with war and death is thought to have endowed this beautiful spring lady with her drooping head which she nods in the knowledge that, for us to appreciate her, it is better we visit her in her own home than have her unhappily visit ours.

BROOM
The yellow-flowered broom was banned from being bought, and barred from houses, during May in case it caused the removal of one of the family, or a friend. Around the West Country the rhyme was known:

> If you sweep the house with blossomed broom in May,
> You'll sweep the head of the house away.

At Whitsuntide (seven weeks after Easter) however, broom was welcomed into the home and used for decoration.

The more sinister sayings were certainly not considered in many rural areas since a bundle of broom, tied with ribbons, often made an appearance at West Country weddings. For any bride the delightful profusion of flowers possessed by broom was regarded as a symbol of good luck and a promise of plenty - revealing its ancient pagan connections with fertility.

COWSLIPS
During the 1940s, when country meadows were still filled with cowslips,

there was a tradition in Gloucestershire of girls weaving a cowslip ball around a roll of grass, until the grass was hidden by the yellow heads of the flower. The ball was tossed from one to another until it was dropped by someone, who then retired from the game. When one of the final pair dropped the cowslip ball the other girl remaining was believed to be the one to marry first among them all. If she gathered the cowslips and placed them under her pillow that night, she would see her future husband in her dreams.

DAFFODILS

Many of the flowers that hang down their heads, daffodils among them, are considered to bring misfortune in their wake if they are taken into a house. It was once considered unlucky in Cornwall to pick garden daffodils while setting poultry but with the coming of commercial daffodil farming fewer people set hens (place broody hens on a clutch of eggs in order to hatch them) and more pick daffodils so a change in the custom could soon come about.

In other areas, like the Severn valley, the number of wild daffodils brought into the house in the first bunch is still said to govern the number of goslings hatched and reared, and to bring only a single bloom into the house was to bring in ill fortune to the goslings.

Daff-a-down-dilly has now come to town,
In a yellow petticoat and a green gown.

The song children sang to greet the daffodil is well known everywhere but almost forgotten is the fact that for many of the singers the appearance of the flower would also remind them that the juice made from its roots would soon be used by their mothers to drop into their ears, since it was a remedy against any 'corrupt filth and running matters in those parts'.

Besides possessing values as an early ear-wax remover the daffodil healed wounds, acted as a purge, strengthened sprains and assisted aches and pains.

DAISIES

It is long-held Devon custom for a maiden to pick daisies by the handful, without looking at them, and use them to divine her own future. With eyes closed she would grasp the flowers until she held a good bundle and only then would she open her eyes. By putting aside one at a time the daisies she has gathered to the repeated refrain "he loves me, he loves me not", she will discover whether the man of her dreams is meant for her.

LADY'S SMOCK

Lady's smock, the flower reserved for the pleasure of fairies, was considered unlucky if brought into the house and was avoided in floral displays of all kinds. If found accidentally used in a May garland or bridal bouquet the arrangement would be burned to avoid disaster striking.

LADY'S MANTLE

Lady's mantle on the other hand was welcome in every home. Used to fill a pillow, this herb will help induce healthy restful sleep, while dewdrops gathered from its folded leaves can be used as a beauty lotion.

Wise women in the Cotswolds prescribed a draft which they derived from the flower for any woman unable to conceive. Throughout the natal period they continued to prescribe the decoction to help the mother retain the child, and to assist her during the birth.

LILIES

In small numbers the lily flower is acceptable but a bed of lilies, or too many seen growing in one garden, would clearly indicate that misfortune, death or disaster was to strike the family. The fragrance of the plant, also known as Our Lady's tears, is so beautiful it is said to be sufficient to draw the nightingale from the hedge and lead him to his chosen mate. Except in Cornwall it would seem, since some say that the nightingale will not even sing there.

MARIGOLDS

A flower of the sun, the marigold, was used in wedding bouquets and love potions and was the symbol of constancy in love and marriage, but in Somerset the picking of marigolds was said to bring thunder during the day. The flower was used in the treatment of smallpox and measles and was said to be helpful for jaundice, and its juice was recommended for sore eyes and the removal of warts.

MYRTLE

Myrtle is, according to floral lore, a married woman's cottage garden companion, and a symbol of married bliss. Following ancient custom the myrtle plant is still used in bridal bouquets today. Taken from a bouquet by a bridesmaid, but never, never, never the bride, sprigs of myrtle continue to be planted in the gardens of newly wed country couples, as long- established tradition has decreed. As the plant struggles to survive, so will the couple also face adversity; as the plant thrives, so will the couple's marriage grow strong; as the bush blossoms, so will the wife be fertile. Myrtle, it is said of in many counties, will only flourish if planted by a good woman and, if a myrtle bush dies, it is a sign of a forthcoming death.

PERIWINKLE

'Sorcerer's violet' was one West Country name for periwinkle; 'blue buttons' was another. But whichever name it was known by, it was a herb regarded to be a good medicine for females and one that may be used to advantage to calm hysterics. It was commonly used as an ingredient in love potions and its properties as a reliable aphrodisiac commended it for regular use. *The Boke of Albertus Magnus* bears witness in detail to the exotic, or erotic use of the delicate flower:

Perywynkle when it is beate unto a powder with worms of ye earth wrapped round it and with an erbe called houselyke it induceth love between man and wife if taken with their meals.

Devon folk gave periwinkle the name 'cut-finger' because of its special medical values as a binder that stemmed the flow of blood.

PRIMROSES

Gloucestershire boys, when learning that primrose roots could be dried and crushed to a fine powder, were not slow to realise that a very effective 'sneezing powder' could be obtained at very little cost. With considerable and increasing interest, these young boys welcomed the season of the primrose - and teachers and parents wondered why.

Primrose powder added to mild snuff has a surprising effect upon old men and the powder, if kept dry, retains its valued properties throughout a whole year, if stocks last that long.

It was also known in Gloucestershire that the primrose has medicinal values. The flowers and leaves, boiled in best lard, produce a cream for healing cuts and chapped hands. The juice of the roots as well as powdered root can be used to induce sneezing. A dram and a half of the dried roots, taken in the autumn, was considered to be a strong but safe emetic.

ROSES

Among the customs of rose care in the West Country there is one that requires that England's favoured national emblem should be pruned on Good Friday, a day dictated by the full moon on or next after 21 March and all young maids who keep to the custom will have the benefit of rose garland guidance to call upon later in the year. A Devon maiden who prunes the rose at moon-ruled Easter time is advised that on midsummer day she should pick a rose while the clock chimes twelve, fold it carefully in white paper, and store the bloom away safely in a drawer for the remainder of the year, untouched again until New Year's Day. She should retrieve the package when she arises on 1 January, and if, when she unwraps the bloom she finds that it is still fresh, she should pin it to her bosom; the man she is to marry she will meet that day and he will attempt to touch the rose, in a gentlemanly way, but will refrain, unless invited. Sadly, however, if the unwrapped rose has died, there is little hope of the maid finding wedded bliss that year.

ROSEMARY

Rosemary is thought, much like the Holy Thorn, to flower at midnight on Twelfth Night and is regarded by many as being the bloom favoured by the Virgin Mary. It is used by people in all counties throughout the West Country to gain protection against spirits, pixies, witches, lightning, to induce good fortune in love, and to ensure success in enterprise.

A maid, placing it under her pillow on the Eve of St Agnes Day (20 January) while making a fervent plea for guidance to the saint could retire to bed in the sure knowledge that she would dream of her future love:

St Agnes, who, to lovers is kind,
I pray ease the troubles of my mind.
In this long night as I do sleep
Show me the love whose heart I'll keep.

The Queen's posy, carried by Her Majesty at the Maundy Day ceremony and made by the official 'Queen's Herbalist', still includes sprigs of rosemary, and thyme: a reminder of the standard remedy and protection against the Plague.

In *The Wonderful Year*, Thomas Decker , a contemporary of Shakespeare, remarked that the Plague had been so bad that, "Rosemary, which had wont to be sold at twelve pence an armful went now at six shillings a handful".

A rosemary bush grown near the cottage or house will protect the inhabitants from any witchcraft harm and can provide at least one welcome remedy useful to some residents: boiled in collected dew, rosemary prevents baldness when the water is used regularly on the hair.

SNOWDROPS

Although it is regarded as a symbol of hope and purity, like many flowers that hang their heads, the snowdrop is said to be an unlucky flower to bring into the house.

In February, if farmers found that their hens had stopped laying, the milk from their cows turned pale and thin, or the butter lost its colour, the snowdrop was sure to take the blame if it were found in the house.

On one special day each winter, the snowdrop's arrival signals the end of that season, and the coming of spring:

The snowdrop, in purest white array,
First rears its head on Candlemas Day.

In the garden, the snowdrop is welcomed, as are the other flowers in the folklore bouquet.

16 Some Winter Days and Summer Ways

There are customs, traditions and lore for every day of the year. For the seasons, the solstice, the equinox, the pagan ways and Christian saint's days, and more.

Soon after what we now know as Hallowe'en (31 October), the Celts celebrated New Year with the lunar festival of Samhain. It was also one of four celebrations they associated with the livestock cycle but, as winter was approaching, insufficient fodder meant that during this festival livestock must be slaughtered, not sacrificed. Ritual fires were lit on the hilltops and feasting and dancing followed. Cattle were killed for the good of the tribe, and the meat was salted and stored. Samhain marked the time when the barriers between this world and the world of the dead were believed to be removed. The dead stirred from their graves to visit the human world, the veil between this world and that of our ancestors was drawn aside to allow contact to be made and we could seek guidance from our ancestors.

The Druids departed but harvest-end ceremonies were still performed, and ritual fires were still lit on hilltops and in open spaces to defeat the powers of evil and to purify the people. The festivities and celebrations of Samhain were still remembered. For three days, time was abolished, and people 'let their hair down'. Men dressed as women, and vice versa, farmers' gates were unhinged and left in ditches, horses were moved to different fields, children knocked on neighbours' doors asking for foods and treats.

Echoing down the passage of time, over two thousand years, doesn't this all sound very familiar? Ancient rites lie hidden behind easily recognised activities that are enjoyed today.

When Christianity began building upon pagan foundations, the emergence of All Hallows Eve (Hallowe'en), All Hallows Day (1 November) and All Saints Day (2 November) conveniently filled a three day time-space previously devoted to ancient custom.

Ritual fire-raising was widespread across the West Country until almost the end of the nineteenth century and some consider that the ritual continues today in the guise of swaling in moorland areas. Supporters of the fire-raising regard swaling as 'traditional' moorland husbandry; opponents say it is dangerous, unnecessary, and has no land 'preservation' value at all. To the Anglo-Saxons, 'swaelen' meant burning. The fixation with fire that lays waste to moorland on the pretext of continuing 'custom and practice' connects us with our pagan past and finds expression in other fire festivals.

Traditionally, it is still acceptable now to light a bonfire on 5 November, only days away from Samhain, the fire festival celebrated long before Guy Fawkes, conveniently for the clergy, arrived on the scene.

At and around the time of Samhain the fire barrels of Ottery St Mary are still trundled through the streets while, in more recent years, the traditional bonfires have been extended to fireshow celebrations. Sticklepath, near Okehampton, has staged a fireshow for over a decade. In North Devon the fireshow has an even longer history.

Our Hallowe'en celebrations have now been debased, some say, by that 'trick or treat' Americanisation, without their knowing of the childish pranks played in West Country towns and villages centuries before the *Mayflower* sailed from Plymouth.

Is it mere coincidence that we remember our illustrious dead, with full pomp and ceremony, on the eleventh day of November, within sight of Samhain?

The pagan feasting that came about to use up every morsel of food, continues through our end-of-year celebrations; except we now stock up food for them. Christmas Eve is an omen- and advice-filled night, for any who care to listen to the 'old' wisdom. If a lamp goes out on Christmas Eve it is an omen of death; but bread baked that night is said never to go mouldy; the song of the robin that eve increases tenfold in volume and sweetness; the pixies of Devon and Cornwall hold services of gladness in sheltered places on the moors; and pumps and wells are filled with wine instead of water. But be warned, they who drink from a pump or at a well, and are aware of the wine, will be instantly struck dead!

Do not be alarmed by the cockerels that crow all through the dead of night before Christmas Day. According to legend they must do so to ensure that: "Each fettered ghost slip to his several grave."

If the crowing cockerels keep you awake then put your sleepless hours to good use and guard the Christmas pie. The pie, according to W Crossing's writings in *Western Antiquary* (1881/82), represented the manger at Bethlehem, and its contents were the offerings made by the three wise men. Herrick records that a solitary watcher guarded a pie throughout the night before Christmas:

Come guard this night the Christmas-pie,
That the thief, though ne'er so sly,
With his flesh-hooks, don't come nigh
To catch it.
From him, who all alone sits there,
Having his eyes still in his ear,
And a deal of nightly fear,
To watch it.

The earliest of Christmas feasts was not the pie, or any of the meats that weighed down tables in medieval days. It was an ancient dish of cree'd hulled wheat, stewed gently for twelve hours or more, then boiled until it jelled. Mixed with milk, sweetened with honey, spiced, and served hot, like porridge, or cold with cream, it was 'frumenty' - probably known and made before humans used iron or put ashen faggots on their fires:

Come, bring with a noise,
My merry, merry boys,
The Christmas log to the firing;
While my good dame, she
Bids ye all be free,
And drink to your hearts' desiring.

With the last year's brand
Light the new block, and
For goodness in his spending
On your psalteries play,
That sweet luck may
Come while the log is a-tending.

Drink now the strong beer,
Cut the white loaf here;
The while the meat is a-shredding
For the rare mince-pie,
And the plums stand by
To fill the paste that's a-kneading.

Known throughout the West Country until quite recently, the Christmas bull held memories of times when going about in animal disguise was a pagan practice at the winter festival.

The Christian Church had tried to suppress all the pagan rites but Caesarius of Arles, in the fifth century, wrote of men dressed in animal costume:

Some who have been baptised put on counterfeit forms and monstrous faces ...
Some are clothed in hides of cattle; others put on the heads of beasts, rejoicing

and exulting that they have so transformed themselves into the shapes of animals that they no longer appear to be men.

Until well into this century, the 'transformed' man was accompanied by wassailers, who went around in groups, particularly at Christmas, to drink to the health and prosperity of their hosts. The wassail bowl, filled with hot spiced drink, was passed around and drinking cups were filled from it. Toasts were proposed, wassail songs sung and sometimes gifts were requested by the wassailers before they left. Custom varied, however. In Tetbury, in the Cotswolds, a wooden, carved bull's head with long horns, shiny eyes and a white face was 'possessed' by one family for generations. At Christmas time, family carol singers carried it round the town and nearby villages, hidden beneath sacking. When cottage doors were opened to them in response to their carols, the sacking was lifted to reveal the Christmas bull.

The Christmas candle, ornamental and of great size, was either lit on Christmas Eve to give light to the supper, or early on Christmas morning, and allowed to burn until night when it was ceremoniously extinguished. It was then relit during the evening on each successive night until Twelfth Night when it was put out for the last time.

As long as the Yule candle burned steadily when it was lit, the home would receive blessings, but if it was blown out by accident during the festival, it was an omen of misfortune for the family. The candle was never 'blown' out at any time, when it was to be extinguished. Instead the wick was pressed with a pair of tongs to stifle the flame, generally by the eldest member of the family.

The Yule candle may not be so readily seen nowadays, but the candle lights on Christmas trees are.

New Year is party time, enjoyed when it is probably cold, wet, snowy or icy, and impeded by nasty weather conditions that might have been avoided if someone long ago had the sense to decide that a 'new' year should start later in the year.

When we gather together with friends to 'see' the New Year in, does anyone remember that our ancestors opened their doors to 'let' the New Year in too ?

In centuries past when people opened their door to welcome in the New Year everyone stepped out of the house holding some money in their left hand, walked away a short distance, changed the money over from their left hand to the right, turned around, and returned to the house again. This ensured that money would continue to enter the house all through the year.

The Dartmoor tradition of opening the door for the 'first comer', quoted in *Western Antiquary* (1881 / 82), describes New Year being welcomed in by a family sitting in silence as midnight approached, in a darkened room with all possible light excluded. As the clock strikes twelve the doors and windows are thrown open wide by the family who peer out into the night anxiously looking for the 'first comer'. If their first visitor is of a dark or swarthy complexion it would be regarded as a good omen and the family could celebrate, but if someone should approach who is fair of hair or pale of face their arrival would betoken serious ill fortune. Today's 'first foot', the first living soul to enter the door on New Year's morning, combines and keeps alive the ancient customs of 'letting in' the New Year and 'gift giving'- the bringing of gifts to ensure that the basic needs of the household are provided for, and poverty avoided.

There were other customs too, earlier ones that didn't rely upon contrived visits. A good wife who tried to keep busy on New Year's Day would be expected to make certain that ashes from the grate were not taken out of the house, to ensure that luck was not taken out with them. Neither would she sweep dust out of a house, or throw water away in case the household luck should depart with it; and to wash clothes on this first day of the year was a certain way to attract bad fortune.

While her parents carefully ushered in the year, concerning themselves with preserving the family fortunes, their daughter, a young Devon maid, would wait with eager anticipation for the first full moon to illuminate the skies after the year began. On the night that the silver globe appeared she would go forth and consult it as custom decreed and, gazing up at its beauty, would say:

All hail to thee moon, all hail to thee
I pray thee good moon, reveal unto me
This night who my future husband will be.

Bowing low in abeyance to the moon the girl would go swiftly to her bed where, in her dreams, the moon would reveal the face of her future life partner.

Like us, our Celtic ancestors celebrated New Year but at a different time of year and not once, but twice. Celtic celebrations for a New Year took place twice in thirteen lunar returns. Beltane (1 May) was the festival they celebrated, according to the moon. The ritual fires were lit, the celebrations began and the summer half of their year was welcomed anew. Samhain (31 October-2 November) celebrated the New Year beginning with winter. Their feasts and festivals and tribal-area-marking, fire-raising, love-invoking, winter rites and summer ritual, all commenced with and followed either Beltane or Samhain, and ours still do.

Over the centuries the pagan festivities were taken over by the churches when the clergy realised that people would not ignore the ways of their ancestors. The spring equinox and summer solstice rituals gave way to Easter and midsummer celebrations; but Easter never lost its links with the moon that still defines the Easter Day.

Across the West Country and throughout Britain, the age-old May Day celebrations continue, for age-old reasons that are now often unknown.

Earlier this century it was a May Day tradition for young girls to carry about dolls, dressed as richly as they could make them, in baskets of flowers;

and in some areas boys carrying garlands of flowers accompanied them. It has been suggested that the custom originally accorded recognition to the Blessed Virgin, patroness of the month of May, or to Flora, the May Queen, while others contend, probably correctly in our opinion, that the Roman virginal goddess of culture known as Minerva, or the Celtic deity Brighid, who became revered by Celtic Christians as Saint Bride, were the subject of this ancient recognition.

There is, however, little doubt that the doll originally represented summer, who was returning to the world to bestow the benefits of fertility and plenty. Tradition decreed that the face of the doll was to be covered over carefully, only to be revealed to those who passed the test of initiation.

In the busy towns or quiet villages the custom of pedestrians being accosted for a coin on Maydoll Day rarely brought anything less than a merry response to a child's plea. Taken in return for a pretty curtsey and the initiation question, "Will you please to see a maydoll?", an acceptable coin was sufficient to ensure the privilege of viewing the concealed figurine. None of the interested, but 'uninitiated', passers-by were permitted to lift the veil which would reveal the babe in the bower until they had qualified themselves for the privilege with appropriate payment. Briefly revealed, and shared with the benefactor, the doll would then be swiftly covered again before the child went skipping away, pursued by her garland-carrying companion to waylay another prospective client to 'initiate'.

The custom of carrying maydolls survived well into the second quarter of the twentieth century. A letter to *The Times* in 1927 describes the custom and informs us that both girls and boys took part in this traditional form of money-making with the boys carrying garlands in the form of short flower-wreathed poles. The writer added that, "expectation is written on their faces, and pennies extracted by each child . . . So far as I can see, it is not etiquette to come out on this quest for pennies after 12 years of age for a girl or 14 for a boy".

> *Round the maypole, trot trit trot*
> *Touch the maypole we have got*
> *Fine and gay*
> *Trot away*
> *Happy on our new May Day.*

The Gloucestershire verse was chanted by innocent children long before words like gay were hijacked but also long after the fertility rites that were associated with the coming of summer had been abandoned. Many other rites were Christianised, but not that one. Maypoles were forbidden throughout the kingdom in 1644, but returned with the King.

In parts of Cornwall it is still the custom for some to hang a piece of furze over their neighbour's door. Their forefathers would have demanded breakfast of bread and cream for having done so but more recently we know that something put in a charity collection box is preferred.

Despite the denunciation by the Puritans of all things pagan, and their particular hatred for the May-time rituals, the celebrations continued with the restoration of the monarchy and games, maze walking, cake and ale making, kissing customs and garland making all flourished.

In Cornwall during the last century the streets of villages and towns were thronged on May Day with children wearing colourful paper clothes, decorated with flowers, and going singing through the streets. In the evening the pagan fire festivals were followed, if not admitted, by bonfires being lit, burning torches used in colourful processions, and fire-games played by daring young men who raced a given distance carrying blazing tar barrels or kicked a burning ball from place to place.

Kingsbridge children carried garlands and bunches of flowers tied to poles around the town, with or without dolls, dancing and singing their way though the streets. Garlands, consisting of two or more intersecting hoops covered in flowers, were popular in Dartmouth, while the weight of the garlands being carried in Salcombe was considerably increased when the number of hoops increased also. The floral globe that was produced became a ball of flowers that taxed the strength of many a child who was encouraged to carry it through the town by proud parents.

In West Country celebrations bright ribbons were always incorporated with the seasonal flowers - kingcups, tulips, cowslips, early roses, wallflowers, polyanthus, and many more that crowded together in garlands or globes.

In some areas the customs of Garland Day have been retained on 13 May, the old May Day, which indicates clearly that customs came before calendars, and in many cases still should.

The ram roast remains part of modern festivities that owes its origins to pagan seasonal celebrations. Eves, feasts and 'saint's' days now acceptably screen off the past. The selection and the sacrificial slaughter may no longer be a visible part of the community celebration but the roasting still remains; and where this has ceased it is likely to have been replaced by the more modern version of the ritual, the barbecue: the sacrificial principles continue.

A South Hams curate made notes in 1853 which drew a comparison between Scottish celebrations of the feast of Beltane, supposed originally to include a sacrifice to Baal, and the revels observed annually in his village below the edge of Dartmoor. Just before daybreak the young men proceeded to the moor to select a male lamb for the revels. On their return, they killed, prepared and roasted the animal.

When the revel roast was ready, risking cut hands as the carvers cut the meat, the young men crowded around, pushing and pulling, struggling and straining, to catch hold of a slice of meat as it was cut clear of the carcass as this they considered would bring them luck for the following year. Having gained their prize and consumed it, as a further act of gallantry the young men fought their way back through the jostling crowds to obtain a slice of ram for their chosen lady who, like all the village maidens, would attend the ram roast revels in her finest dress.

And to such revels came dancers long ago with, as Junius wrote, "faces blackened by soot that they might better pass for moors". Their dances, first supposed to have been brought into England when John of Gaunt returned from Spain during the reign of Edward III, are now believed to have concealed their pagan origins for centuries.

The fertility rites performed to ensure a safe increase in animal births, the productivity values of land, and the successful growing of crops were vital to our ancestors and dance, like word of mouth, has been a worldwide communication since pagan times.

Few dancers among modern morris teams, or sides as they are called, would know how to service a cow, prepare the land or raise a crop, but their dances still inspire.

Dancers were certainly thriving in south Devon during the sixteenth century, and were obviously considered to be of value to a community. Their country rates may have varied slightly but in Worth's *History of Plymouth* the costs for the dancers at city celebrations are recorded thus:

1566; Item payde to the Mynstrills and Dauncers upn Maye daie for theire dynner and drynkinge, 6s 8d. [approx 34p].

1668; Item pd, for dressinge of the Maye Pole, 1s 0d [5p]. Item pd, for rentinge of the Maye Pole 3s 4d. Item pd, to the Morishe Daunseres on Maye daye, 4s 0d [20p]. Item pd, to Kympe for the Maye Pole, 3s 4d [17p].

All Hallows Day was commemorated in May until AD834. It was a festival devoted to a noble white-robed army of ancient martyrs, and Celtic crosses were still paraded by boys in the mid-twentieth century accompanied by other boys blowing horns. This noisy ritual derived from the doctrine of resurrection that was taught by Celtic missionaries from the sixth century and encouraged the use of horns and trumpets to awaken those who 'sleep'. The achievements gained by horn blowing are recorded and documented, and were far longer remembered and recognised. Noise enough "to waken the dead" is a phrase not uncommonly used, even today.

Until almost the end of the last century, across the quiet South Hams countryside May Day morn was greeted by a hideous cacophony of sound that rent the air from daybreak. Gangs of boys would be up and out at first light, parading vigorously around, producing an awful noise from cow-horns and tin trumpets which frightened their foes and offended their families, and was far from melodious. The trumpets did make sweet music to the ears of the pedlars who swiftly departed from Dartmouth, kept clear of Kingsbridge, slipped out of Salcombe, and made for the moors after selling them to eager 'players'.

The 'music' the 'players' produced is claimed to have been needed since ancient times to ensure that everyone was aware that summer had returned. There were however some who made an alternative claim. Those who were wise to the ways of Devon's witches suggested that the lusty performance was required to efficiently banish any witch remaining in the area after the previous night's (Walpurgis) Sabbat.

The merry bands of music makers were permitted entry into houses, homes and cottages across the southern county; the houses, homes and cottages of the more gullible that is. For, when displaying their less than musical abilities in the bedrooms of late risers, the boys would invariably, and hardly surprisingly, find themselves rewarded with coins to ensure that they immediately departed to share their glad tidings that 'summer-is-a-cumin'-in', with another neighbour or, with sufficient financial inducement, with another neighbourhood.

Every year continues, day by day, unfolding to the folklore known in ages past and tempered by the present times. Shakespeare alluded often to the values of timeless traditions, rural remedies and the ways of the wise ones in the countryside. These sentiments he expressed in *As You Like It*:

> ... *Hath not old custom made this life more sweet*
> *Than that of painted pomp ?*
> *Are not these woods more free from peril than the envious court?*
> ... *Sweet are the uses of adversity;*
> *Which, like the toad, ugly and venomous,*
> *Wears yet a precious jewel in his head;*
> *And this our life exempt from public haunt,*
> *Finds tongues in trees, books in the running brooks,*
> *Sermons in stones, and good in everything.*
>   *I would not change it.*

Further Reading

Albertus Magnus, St *The Boke of Albertus Magnus* (c 1270)

Baring-Gould, Rev S *Curious Myths of the Middle Ages* (1869; New Orchard Editions 1987)

Crossing, W *Western Antiquary* (1881/82)

Culpeper, Nicholas *Complete Herbal* (1653; W Foulsham & Co)

Ellis, William *Modern Husbandman, vols i,v,vii,viii* (1750)

Farming Press *TV Vet Book for Farmers* (1964)

Gerard, John *The Herball or Generall Historie of Plantes* (John Norton 1597)

Hamilton Jenkin, A K *Cornwall and its People* (J M Dent & Sons Ltd 1945)

Herrick, Thomas *The Poems of Herrick Thomas* (TC & EC Jack)

Hone, William *The Every Day Book* (Thomas Tegg 1826)

Howitt, William *The Rural Life of England* (Longman, Orme, Brown & Green 1840)

Hunt, Robert (ed) *Popular Romances of the West of England* (facsimile of 1881 ed, Llanerch Publishing 1993)

Long, George *The Folklore Calendar* (Philip Allan, 1930)

Plinius Secundus *Historia Naturalis* (c AD 75, trans Philemon Holland)

Porteous, Alexander *Forest Folklore* (George Allan & Unwin 1928)

Radford, E & M A Encyclopedia of Superstitions (Rider & Co)

Raymond, Walter *The Book of Simple Delights*

St Leger-Gordon, Ruth *The Witchcraft and Folklore of Dartmoor* (1965, reprinted Peninsula Press 1994)

Swan, John *The Folk Lore & Speculum Mundi* (1643)

Swainson, Rev C *The Folk Lore and Provincial Names of British Birds* (Elliot Stock 1886)

Tusser, Thomas *Five Hundred Points of Good Husbandrie* (1931 ed)

Whitworth, Belinda *A Glimpse of Dartmoor Folklore* (Peninsula Press 1992)

Worth, R N *History of Plymouth* (W Brendon & Son 1873)